CLIENT RELATIONSHIP MANAGEMENT

Using Relationship Management and Project Service Excellence to Create a Competitive Advantage

David A. Po-Chedley

HRD Press   Amherst   Massachusetts

Copyright © 2001 David Po-Chedley

Published by Human Resource Development Press, Inc.
22 Amherst Road
Amherst, Massachusetts 01002

1-800-822-2801 (U.S. and Canada)
1-413-253-3488
1-413-253-3490 (fax)
http://www.hrdpress.com

ISBN 0-87425-637-2

Production services by CompuDesign
Cover design by Eileen Klockars
Editorial services by Robie Grant

Dedication

To Eileen—my wife, my best friend, my source of support and inspiration, and the wonderful mother of our son, Liam.

Acknowledgments

Several people have played essential roles in this book. Carla Queen provided the initial idea to develop this content into a book. Wes Sager provided substantial input and ideas that made the book possible. Cyndi Lagasse and Deborah Storti played important roles in the development and editing process. Chris Hunter from HRD Press helped us navigate the publishing process. I owe each of these people a debt of gratitude for their contribution and support.

CONTENTS

INTRODUCTION

"An idea can turn to dust or magic,
depending on the talent that rubs against it."

—William Bernbach
Advertising Executive

Welcome to Client Relationship Management. The objectives of this book are to:

- Provide you with information and techniques to turn your client relationship skills into a competitive advantage
- Review and apply tools that will promote consistent, well-planned, and personalized client interaction

This book is designed to help you build strong relationships as you manage projects by:

1. Clearly understanding the contribution of service performance and the four dimensions of relationship management to project success

2. Appreciating the importance of defining a solution that is based on the client's history, addresses the needs of all key stakeholders, and meets the criteria for exceeding client expectations

3. Designing a plan that secures ownership from stakeholders, delivers the solution within realistic limits, and encourages team collaboration

4. Promoting project implementation through solid stakeholder commitment, strong communication, and well-managed hand-offs

5. Orchestrating project closeout that confirms customer satisfaction, acknowledges individual and team performance, and highlights best practices and lessons learned

✳

6. Creating a Service Plan to ensure attention to your client's implicit expectations and deliverables, and to heighten focus on the "How" aspects of service performance

KEY TOOLS AND ORGANIZERS

As you read this book, you'll encounter several tools designed to organize and enhance your relationship with the client.

Each tool is directed at a critical component of the relationship. Use of the tools will promote careful planning and management of key client interactions, moving the effort forward smoothly and without mishap. The results will be glowing testimonials and/or repeat business.

Each tool is introduced and demonstrated within a chapter in which it is commonly put to effective use. Keep in mind, however, that these tools are quite versatile and some can make a valuable contribution in all chapters.

Also remember that all tools may not be appropriate for all client projects. Use only those tools that will add value to your relationship with each client.

- **Decision Matrix:**
    - The goal of the Decision Matrix is to establish relationships with key stakeholders at the right time, and to ensure they have the information they need to ensure a favorable decision.
    - The desired outcome is a timely decision promoting the progress of the project and contributing to client satisfaction.
- **Stakeholder Analysis:**
    - The goal of the Stakeholder Analysis is to ensure that the right people are involved at the right time along the way, and

to develop relationships that will foster their support and buy-in for the project.

- The desired outcome is smooth progress of the project with a minimum of resistance from stakeholders.

- **Presentation Guide:**

    - The goal of the Presentation Guide is to gather information on the "buying habits" and communication preferences of the target group.

    - The desired outcomes are successful presentations that quickly earn the target group's commitment and advance their relationship with the team.

- **Communication Matrix:**

    - The goal of the Communication Matrix is to document what information stakeholders desire, when they want it, and how they want to receive it.

    - The desired outcome is satisfied stakeholders, minimal project delays, and efficient decision making.

- **Relationship Extension Plan:**

    - The goal of the Relationship Extension Plan is to identify additional opportunities to serve your satisfied client.

    - The desired outcome is the solidification of a long-term loyalty between client and supplier, and ongoing commitment to manage the relationship, even after the technical aspects of the project have been completed.

TIPS AND REMINDERS

At the beginning of each chapter, you will find a list of tips and reminders designed to enhance client relationships. Some of them involve application of concepts and tools described in the corresponding chapter. Others are simple, quick ideas that can be applied independent of the content of the book. In either case, it is strongly recommended that you apply these tips and reminders in a flexible fashion. That is, use only those that will enhance a given client relationship. It's important to recognize that what works for one client may not work well with another.

APPLICATION MATRIX

The Application Matrix is described in Chapter 6. After you have reviewed the content in the previous chapters, this tool will help you to develop your own customized application plan for the content of the book that best suits your needs. The concepts, tips, reminders, and tools can then be applied in a way that will be most beneficial to you and your clients.

Reminder: While the project will be the vehicle used to present and discuss all the content in this book, most of the tools, tips, and reminders are also applicable to nonproject relationships as well.

Chapter One

1

The Client Relationship

CLIENT RELATIONSHIP MANAGEMENT

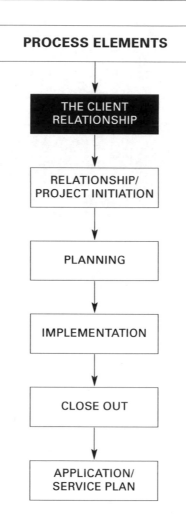

PROCESS ELEMENTS

THE CLIENT RELATIONSHIP

RELATIONSHIP/ PROJECT INITIATION

PLANNING

IMPLEMENTATION

CLOSE OUT

APPLICATION/ SERVICE PLAN

| WHAT? | ✓ The Client Relationship |

| WHY? | ✓ To clarify the dimensions of the client relationship and the factors that impact client satisfaction. |

| HOW? | ✓ Understand the First Law of Service
✓ Understand the dimensions of client relationships
✓ Review factors that cause projects to fail |

| KEY TOOLS | ✓ Tips and Reminders |

CLIENT RELATIONSHIP BUILDING QUESTIONS

✓ What are the factors that impact the level of client satisfaction?

✓ What are the dimensions of client relationships?

✓ What causes projects to fail?

ADDITIONAL QUESTIONS

✓ _____

✓ _____

✓ _____

RELATIONSHIP BUILDING TIPS AND REMINDERS

1. Deliver communications using media that is client-friendly (i.e., find out if hard copy, fax, e-mail, etc., is best for them).
2. Know your client's first choices for meeting locations and communication media.
3. Encourage all team members to adopt high standards of professionalism while remaining authentic and natural toward clients.
4. Know when to employ control, influence, or adherence in managing client relationships.
5. Be sure the client knows all the ways to reach you (phone, fax. e-mail, etc.).
6. Respond immediately to a client's message if you have the answer, but never take more than one business day to respond.
7. Be aware of your own style and preferences so you can comfortably adjust to the style and preferences of your client.
8. Treat internal clients with exactly the same service standards as external clients.
9. Keep the implicit dimensions of service performance on a par with the explicit dimensions of technical performance.
10. Ensure that all clients are addressed appropriately (first or surnames, titles, etc.).

REFERENCE MATERIAL

&

APPLICATION GUIDELINES

✳ **8**

PROJECT CLIENTS AND "OTHERS"

Everyone in your organization has a responsibility to serve and support clients. Clients come in many definitions, including:

External Clients:

- *Paying Project Clients:* These are the most obvious clients you work for, and usually the most important. But don't make the mistake of assuming they are the only clients in the project life cycle.

- *Vendors & Suppliers:* Though we most often think of ourselves as clients of these groups, we often need to provide them with information, guidance, feedback, etc. In that moment, they are our clients.

- *The Community:* Socially responsible organizations are initiating a variety of environmental, volunteer, and stewardship projects in the local communities. Anyone who benefits, directly or indirectly, from these initiatives is your client.

Internal Clients:

- *Cross-Functional Peers:* Every member of the team will serve as both supplier and client as the project unfolds. When you provide something to a peer, you're a supplier. When you receive something, you're a customer.

- *Your Superiors:* Project stakeholders are very important clients, as are managers whose functional areas will be impacted by the project outcomes.

- *Your Staff:* You must deliver resources, information, direction, priorities, etc., to anyone you delegate to or whose time you manage.

The way you relate to internal clients is a pretty good indication of how you will relate to your external clients. Be careful to develop and maintain dependable and effective relationships with internal clients or your results for project clients will suffer.

Consider this scenario at Silo International. Everyone in the operations group knows when the end of the quarter arrives: the VP of Operations can be found pounding on the Controller's door for the latest financial reports. The Controller's lack of concern for satisfying her client's needs (providing the VP with fiscal information) can trickle down through the organization as a model, or service standard, for how Silo employees treat their external customers. The connection between the Controller's limited respect for customer service and falling revenues will most likely never be identified.

Similarly, if a project leader repeatedly ignores e-mails or messages from team members, you may see the turnaround time between a customer's inquiry and the team's response getting longer and longer. Team members feel undervalued by the team leader, and in turn, they undervalue the customer. Customer relationships erode, and business ultimately declines.

Just try to remember that whenever your goal is to deliver *anything* to another individual or group, you are the supplier *in a relationship* with a client. You now have the opportunity to advance the relationship and set (or maintain) high standards for others by providing great service.

THE FIRST LAW OF SERVICE

In "Managing the Professional Service Firm," David Maister offers a simple yet universal formula for predicting a client's level of satisfaction. To understand the formula you first must appreciate this prediction:

> Your clients will tend to focus as intensely on the quality of the *service* as they do on the quality of the *work*.

For example, you might be the world's most talented jeweler, but if you deliver a Valentine's pendant on February 15th, the beauty of the craftsmanship will be secondary. Or, if you are the most brilliant lawyer in a criminal courtroom, but don't offer your client any respect or common courtesy, your client list will be far shorter than it should be.

The First Law of Service is this:

SATISFACTION = PERCEPTION minus EXPECTATION

All three components inherent in the First Law of Service are driven by a combination of "what" you deliver and "how" it is delivered.

If your clients' perception of what you delivered is lower than their expectation (i.e., the delivery they had "in mind"), negative satisfaction results.

If, however, your clients' perception of the value you delivered exceeds their expectation, you have created a positive level of satisfaction. The more their perception is above their expectation, the happier they are.

A key aspect of this formula is that all three elements are subjective. You can effectively manage these subjective measurements throughout the project cycle. Doing so will ensure client satisfaction, and develop into a significant competitive advantage.

Imagine you are an internal training consultant for a fast growing financial services firm. The manager of the newest satellite office has requested that you pay a visit so you can train his new operations team in interoffice communications and systems procedures. Aware that this is an "ASAP" situation (and an opportunity to proactively meet urgent needs), you contact the branch manager to explore options for addressing her plan. You arrange for an advance "Q/A Conference Call" with the staff to orient them to your upcoming visit; an e-mail bulletin board for "as needed" input; and a flight 2 days earlier to move up the training event. Utilizing direct communications and creative scheduling, you have exceeded the manager's expectations and demonstrated your skills as a relationship manager.

Technical vs. Service Performance

Moving up from "technically proficient project manager" to "project professional" requires more than the ability to deliver results. It requires an understanding of implicit as well as explicit client needs.

Project clients differentiate a project deliverable from the manner in which the item was delivered.

A project deliverable (product or service) is the result of your team's "technical performance." These explicit project results are the "what" you have agreed to produce as a result of the project.

The manner in which the project outcome is delivered is your team's "service performance." This is the implicit dimension of the project, and is reflected in the "how" of the delivery.

Whereas the project client depends on the explicit project outcome to achieve business results, the client experiences the implicit service component of the project. For most of us, the experience of a consumer exchange usually outlives the usefulness of the deliverable itself.

If you engage the services of a talented tax preparer, who charges reasonable fees and reduces your tax obligation, you automatically return next year, right? The answer is a resounding Yes, *unless* the planner didn't return your calls, made you feel ignorant or incompetent, and used explanations filled with tax code technicalities and complicated formulas. The benefits of what he did are overshadowed by how he treated you. Similarly, your clients will remember *how* you provided service long after you complete the delivery of the project outcomes.

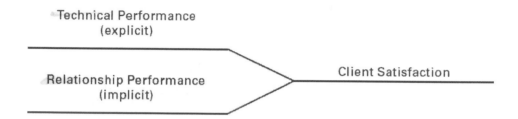

Technical Performance (explicit)

Relationship Performance (implicit)

Client Satisfaction

It's not possible to address one without the other because:

■ The project is the context within which relationships are developed

■ Relationships are impacted by the way the project is managed

■ The project will be managed in a way that reflects the quality of the relationships

What Clients Notice

Every interaction with your client represents a "moment of truth." That is, each time you interact, your clients pay attention to everything you do and say. In most cases, they won't comment on what they see or hear. The sum total of all these interactions represents how they see you. It also represents how they are likely to describe you to others (including prospective clients).

Your clients pay attention to:

Professionalism: If you or your workplace are clean and neat, this reflects positively on you. If you speak clearly and appropriately to the situation (e.g., no slang, jargon, acronyms the client doesn't understand), your client will notice. Finally, if you maintain a positive attitude, this will be noticed by your clients.

Communication: Your ability to ask the right questions at the right time are critical to successful communication with the client. So too is your ability to tell clients what they need to know at the right time.

Availability and Responsiveness: Your clients will appreciate it if you are there when they need you. They will also appreciate timely responses to their calls, questions, etc.

Understanding Expectations: If you take the time to clearly understand their needs (i.e., around quality, value, timeliness, etc.), they will understand that you actually care about them.

Product/Service Knowledge: Your ability to speak intelligently about your products, your services, and your organization will impact your clients' confidence in you, and ultimately, their interest in working with you.

Managing Client Problems: If you can prevent most client problems from happening, you're well ahead in the game. Equally important, when problems do arise, you need to be able to manage them in a way that shows the client that you are well prepared to deal with difficult situations.

Under-Promise & Over-Deliver

The more successful you are at maintaining a realistic expectation for the deliverable, the greater will be the positive differential between perception and expectation. To manage client expectations:

- Be conservative: set realistic expectations
- If the delivery schedule must change, immediately involve the client in setting new dates
- Define the minimum deliverable you can produce and plan to exceed it

The more successful you are at delivering your product or service in a style, manner, or method that pleases or impresses your clients, the higher will be their perception of overall project outcomes. You can increase perceived value by:

- Holding to all milestones and delivery dates
- Knowing your client's preferences for deliveries and communications
- Surprising your client with some extra deliverables and added value

Imagine you have taken a VCR in for repair, and have been told to call back in 3 to 4 weeks. How would you react if the repair shop called you in 10 days, said the unit was not only repaired but cleaned as well, and they would drop it off after a service call to someone in your neighborhood! The extra cost and effort for the shop is minimal. Combining technical expertise (the repair) with service performance (the delivery) to exceed your expectations is very effective in raising your level of satisfaction. Your project clients will appreciate and remember your efforts to bring added value to the relationship.

Delivering added value, and maximizing client satisfaction, is much more than good luck. Constantly monitoring the variables in the First Law of Service will result in:

- More future business
- Client testimonials
- Increased referrals
- Client loyalty (it is far cheaper to keep a client than to get a new one)

Relationships Matter Pre- and Post-Sale

Most of the projects you work on, and most of the examples in this workshop, are focused on deliverables for existing clients. The project has been defined as a result of a sale, the extension of an existing relationship, or to meet internal business goals (working with internal clients). But there is a huge pre-sale world out there, and relationship management can make the difference between getting the contract or losing the business.

Sales representatives in every industry are keenly aware that competition is intensifying and consumer choice is growing rapidly. Long-distance carriers, rental cars, stock trading services, and pet supplies—our choices are endless. The products we can purchase are becoming more numerous and similar. The services that surround our purchase, and the way the supplier relates to us, are quickly becoming the differentiating factors.

Consumers are seeking the supplier who can deliver the goods, *and* a reliable relationship. If the sales rep can prove that she understands the consumer's need, and can position her product as a total solution for the need, chances are she will get the order. Knowing, and relating to, the individual consumer is much more important than industry knowledge and demographic data.

The same holds true for team-based selling. Consumers want to see depth and dependability in their suppliers, especially when a long-term commitment is on the table. Professional services firms, construction companies, and distribution networks are examples of suppliers who become partners with their clients, not simply vendors. They must approach a sale as a project, from definition through close out, and prove they have the best technical and service performance in the industry. Sales teams need to demonstrate healthy relationships among themselves in order to establish relationships based on confidence with their prospects.

THE FOUR DIMENSIONS OF RELATIONSHIP MANAGEMENT

To truly excel at satisfying client needs, you must be aware of and involved in the four dimensions of relationship management. These dimensions are:

- Intrapersonal
- Interpersonal
- Team Dynamics
- Cultural/Operational

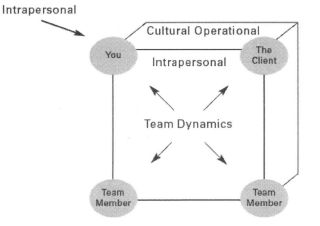

We will explain each of the four dimensions of relationship management separately in the next section. We can artificially delineate and define them for discussion purposes, but we cannot isolate them in the real world of relationships. Each dimension is constantly impacting and influencing the other dimensions—they are all interdependent on each other.

Consider the dynamics of a baseball team, with you as the left fielder.

You're the One

Intrapersonally speaking, you are responsible for development of your athletic skills and your attitude relative to the game. And although these traits are specific to you and you alone, they can impact other aspects of the game. For example, if you are faster than the right fielder, the pitcher may throw pitches to intentionally draw fly balls to your field, feeling you are more likely to make the outs. In addition, if you demonstrate an energetic and contagious attitude for winning, the coach may play you despite the fact you have a lower batting average than the other left fielders, due to the positive impact you have on team morale.

It Takes Two

Have you ever seen two fielders collide as they chase a long fly ball? Their lack of interpersonal familiarity or communication results in a base hit for the opponent, and has a negative impact for the entire team. Even though the rest of the team is powerless to influence the outcome of this two-player event, they are nonetheless all affected by it.

What a Play!

Have you ever seen a triple play? It is that rare but exciting collaboration when several players act as if they were technically choreographed to execute the play. It calls for acute awareness and anticipation of where your teammates will be, as well as your role in pulling off a perfectly coordinated team play. Though nonverbal, this is a true demonstration of putting relationships to work at solving a problem.

The Powerful Intangibles

And finally, why is home field advantage such a powerful aspect of team competition? It is a cultural issue. The home team is familiar with the idiosyncrasies of their field, used to the climate, comfortable in their own clubhouse, and certainly pumped up by the crowd. They "know the ropes," the vendors, the reporters, and the die-hard fans. And given the feeling of belonging, they can focus on their performance.

So, from individual ability to the emotion of hometown cheers, team success is a constant integration of intrapersonal, interpersonal, team, and cultural factors. Your relationships with yourself, a peer, your group, and your environment can work for or against your project success.

Dimension One: Intrapersonal Awareness

This dimension is the degree to which you appreciate your personal style and preferences. This is the first step in understanding how your personality affects *how* you work, *relate* to others on the team, and *enjoy* your work.

Intrapersonal awareness is not about assessing individual beliefs or core values. It is about understanding how your beliefs and values affect your behavior, and how your behavior impacts others.

A popular way to develop a picture of your personality preferences is the *Meyers-Briggs Type Indicator (MBTI)*. Such tools don't suggest that some personality types are more successful than others; just that awareness of differences can improve results.

For example, if you rank high as an extrovert, you enjoy social events with a lot of people. Don't take your introverted client to a loud club full of strangers.

Or, if you are a visual learner, don't assume that your client will get the most information from your PowerPoint demo. A simple verbal description may be far more effective.

Behavioral Styles: Influence and Conflict Management

A key element of the relationship management process is your ability to manage differences. During any project, it is inevitable that differences and conflict will surface between you and the client, as well as between team members. In both cases, understanding the various styles used for managing differences and conflict will help you to exert positive influence without alienating the client and/or team members.

Individuals bring their strengths, weaknesses, assumptions, attitudes, and beliefs to bear in the management of influence and conflict. These elements of personal behavior are reflected in the way we act and react to others in conflict situations.

A useful way to observe and describe conflict management styles is to consider the two dimensions that contribute most to our observable behavior.

1. **Task/activity orientation**—This represents our concern for the activity at hand and how we strive to accomplish our goals in the most effective, productive, and efficient manner. In its various forms, it represents the bottom line, results, profit, total service rendered, etc.

2. **People/relationship orientation**—Regardless of the task involved, the people asked to accomplish it can be expected to have unique individual needs and desires. Their motivation to accomplish the task in an excellent manner will hinge in part on the level of concern that others, particularly those that lead them, show for their individual needs.

We can represent the most typical conflict management styles as follows:

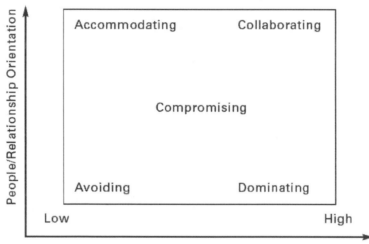

Description of Influence and Conflict Management Styles:

1. **Dominating** individuals view differences or conflict as a threat to their authority and control, thus it is important to cut it off as quickly as possible. This frequently involves the use of intimidation, threats, and personal attacks. Dominating individuals usually take a fixed position and refuse to deviate from it. Their

win-lose perception of situations makes it difficult for them to back down after a conflict has emerged.

2. **Accommodating** individuals view differences or conflict as a potentially devastating blow to the warmth and friendly atmosphere that they strive to maintain; thus, they actively avoid it. Accommodating individuals quickly yield in most confrontations, but if conflict is unavoidable, they attempt to smooth over the issues so as not to hurt anyone's feelings.

3. When **Avoiding** individuals sense the emergence of differences or conflict, they quickly withdraw in an attempt to avoid the situation altogether. When confronted, they use vague generalizations in an effort to avoid taking a position that might stimulate further conflict.

4. Depending on the situation, **Compromising** individuals deal with differences or conflict in a variety of ways. If unsure of the party line, they avoid or smooth over conflict. If majority thinking and opinion are clear, they more readily accept and, at times, even seek out conflict. Conflict resolution comes primarily from negotiation and majority rule.

5. **Collaborating** individuals view differences or conflict as a tool that, when properly managed, can encourage new and better ideas to emerge. They also realize that conflict can be dysfunctional. They use communication as a useful tool to manage conflict by getting issues out in the open. They seek to resolve underlying causes by confronting the situation in its early stages.

Each of these approaches represents a functioning style that can be observed to varying degrees in every organization. Each is associated with an approach to behavior and interaction that has predictable results.

Receiving Feedback

Whenever communication takes place, various factors are present. In addition to logic and rational thought, people have emotions that enter into communication transactions. We try to take this feeling factor into account when preparing and giving feedback. It is also important in a team environment to anticipate our responses when we are the recipients of feedback. Consider the general responses to feedback in relation to the conflict management styles:

- Dominating: Because this style is characterized by a need for control, it is often difficult for a dominating style person to receive feedback without responding defensively.

- Accommodating: A person with accommodating style may give a silent or aquiescent response to receiving feedback. Accommodaters may take on more responsibility for project problems or issues than is warranted instead of engaging in dialogue during a feedback session.

- Avoiding: A person with an avoiding style may also avoid receiving feedback. When confronted this person will often acknowledge the feedback and then quickly try to move the conversation along to other topics. This can make it more difficult to partner on finding workable solutions.

- Compromising: A person with a compromising style will usually hear feedback, accept some level of responsibility, and look for a middle ground to move the project along. However, this may not provide the most creative or effective solution.

- Collaborating: A person with collaborating style generally seeks to listen carefully to feedback, attempts to determine its validity and the appropriate responsibility level, and pushes forward to effective resolution. Collaborative style and attitude lend themselves to making the best use of feedback when it is offered.

Receiving Feedback Guidelines and Suggestions

Generally speaking, careful listening is the key to making the best use of feedback. The most effective response to feedback is always the one that helps clarify the issue in such a way that it can be resolved quickly and successfully.

Some responses to feedback that can help clarify and resolve issues include:

Silence—Listening quietly, observing, and trying to understand the full message in the feedback.

Acknowledgment—Giving verbal indications of understanding and validation for the feedback.

Inviting nonverbals (as opposed to the "are you crazy?" facial expression)—Using expressions that invite additional information and feedback.

Paraphrasing—Restating the message as you understand it to check the accuracy of the communication.

Active listening—Expressing understanding of the importance of the message, as well as your feelings about it.

Perhaps the most important guideline for receiving feedback is to keep in mind the overall objective of the team and the project. If all parties keep mutual success in the forefront of communication, both the giving and receiving of feedback serves a vital purpose.

Dimension Two: Interpersonal Relationship Management

All of your internal and external clients need to be assured that you:

- Take a genuine interest in them
- Know and respect their preferences
- Will address their needs in a way that is familiar and comfortable to them

Whereas the Golden Rule suggests you should treat others the way YOU would like to be treated, a more accurate piece of advice is to treat others the way THEY want to be treated. It is a natural tendency to assume that what is good enough for us will be good enough for our clients.

How can you determine your client's preferences and comfort zones?

Observation of Behavior

- Be mindful of how your clients choose to communicate with you, and reciprocate whenever possible.
    - Do they send more e-mails or make more phone calls?
    - Do they like face-to-face meetings or do they defer to more efficient exchanges?

Check Out the Client's Workplace

- If a client's office is full of family pictures, it's a pretty safe bet he or she enjoys a question or two about home life. If the office is all files and flowcharts, better stick to business.
- Draw clues from the surroundings the person has chosen to live with for 40 hours each week, and use those clues to pick a communication style.

Ask Questions

- It is perfectly appropriate to ask clients a set of focused questions to plan and implement a strategy for servicing them. This is the basis for the "Service Plan" which follows.

Request Feedback

- Periodically, ask clients to discuss the things you have done that they really enjoyed, and the things they wish you had done differently. Make adjustments accordingly.

Ask questions like:

- "Was the delivery of the report after lunch okay, or would you prefer the next one in the morning?"
- "I assumed you would like invitations to all review meetings. Is that correct? How will I learn of your plan to attend?"

Seek Input from Others

- Chances are you know other people who have a deeper experience with the client than you do, or perhaps with the client's department or company. Collect as much information as you can on what has or hasn't worked. There is no substitute for lessons learned.

One vital aspect of your response to any of the issues above is that the behavior you exhibit to the client is *natural and authentic*. If clients feel you are mimicking them, or making artificial and patronizing gestures, they will resent your efforts.

Do Things with, Not to or for, Your Client

Another aspect of your behavior that contributes to successful relationship management is remembering that you are doing things WITH the client, not TO or FOR them. Sometimes we can view the task of making a delivery, returning a call, or editing a report as an imposed requirement or obligation. In fact, you are entering an interaction (responding to a client need) and you must demonstrate your willingness to actively participate in the solution.

Consider an example. Your client asks you for eight more copies of a lengthy proposal so she can distribute them to her department.

One option is to begrudgingly make the copies and deliver them to her office. Your feelings of being treated like a copy clerk will likely come through and taint the exchange.

Another option is to call the client and offer assistance in the distribution. Perhaps you can send the proposal by e-mail to her staff or provide an electronic copy on a common server for convenient, shared access.

If you still end up making the copies, you will have demonstrated a spirit of cooperation and desire to serve.

Dimension Three: Team Dynamics

As soon as one more person joins your team, you have entered the more complicated world of team dynamics. Where there was only one relationship to manage (between you and the client), now there are three (you and the client, you and your team member, and the other team member and the client).

All the Rules of Relationship Management Still Apply

Even though you are now a member of a team, most of your interactions will be with one other person at any given time. Therefore, keep all the suggestions above in mind for every other person in the team, all the time. When you are interacting with any one of them as your client, he or she is the most important person in the project at that moment.

Define and Acknowledge Interdependencies

Teams have a common goal, and interdependent relationships must develop in order to attain that goal *efficiently*. Everyone will perform better if these aspects of team dynamics are addressed:

- Individual roles are clearly defined and communicated
- Hand-offs are defined, scheduled, and documented
- Communications are thorough and consistent among team members
- Review meetings involve the right people and are efficiently conducted
- Supplier/Client relationships are acknowledged
- Conflicts are surfaced and resolved

Dimension Four: Cultural/Operational Considerations

In order to develop and maintain positive interactions with your clients, you need to be aware of the influence the culture can have on those interactions.

Cultures can impact client interactions in several ways:

- Explicit and implicit codes of conduct (e.g., How does the culture view gifts to clients? What level of confidentiality must be maintained?)
- Communication protocols—formal and informal (e.g., Are all communications documented? Do certain types of communication require approval? When are clients copied on team communication?)
- Image management (e.g., Is there a dress code when meeting with clients? Is there a standard format and package for delivery of reports or other client communications?)

When the project is directed at an external client, you will be dealing with all the issues above times two. It is equally important to be familiar with the cultural issues of your organization and those of your client.

The culture of a business is evident in how it operates in addition to issues related to conduct, image, and communication. Standards or cultural norms established by an organization's operations can have a direct impact on relationships and client interactions.

Administration: Does the client culture call for centralized or decentralized administration? Do administrative functions influence or simply respond to the activities of the business's core functions? Your awareness of the role administration plays in your client's culture can help you relate to administrative stakeholders as well as better manage the role administration plays in the project.

Policies: How traditional is the client culture? Do they allow flextime? How do they handle maternity leave (for mothers *and* fathers)? Is the organization chart vertical or horizontal? Awareness of policy platforms like these will give you valuable clues on how to relate to your clients' work habits and expectations. It is not your place to take a position regarding client policies, but to build your knowledge of them into your service plan for the client.

Infrastructure: Infrastructure can include everything from an on-site cafeteria to voice mail technology to the number of office locations involved in your project. Your awareness of each infrastructure issue can be an opportunity for you to cater to your client. If voice mail is awkward or unreliable, make a concerted effort to use more e-mail or fax deliveries. If team members are located in multiple offices, establish a system for conference calls or electronic conferencing. Make the infrastructure a *known and defined* asset or constraint, and adjust your relationship strategies accordingly.

Capacity: Capacity issues for project execution usually refer to the number of person-hours that can be applied to the project. Capacity limits can be a shortage of people or a build-up of projects. In either case, your role is to be sensitive to the outlay of time your clients (and stakeholders) can realistically afford, and then set a schedule that reflects attainable goals. As a relationship manager, you want people meeting their objectives more often than not. Working towards a well-balanced allocation of resources will make the project experience more enjoyable for everyone and more likely to result in a satisfied client.

Keep in mind that most of the ways cultures impact relationships are through the implementation of unwritten rules. It is important that you request clarification of a cultural issue if you are not certain what is expected of you. Most clients will be quite comfortable explaining the ropes to you in advance, to avoid getting all tangled up in them.

For example, it may be considered disrespectful to show up unannounced in some offices, whereas in others, it is a sign of open and proactive team participation. A simple question before the first visit will let you know whether to call ahead to your client. And, just asking the question is further confirmation that you are genuinely interested in understanding and serving their needs, a key element in solidifying your developing relationship.

CONTROL, INFLUENCE, AND ADHERENCE

When managing relationships, you will often make an individual impact, and other times need to go with the flow.

You have the greatest degree of **control** over your own behavior, both in how you conduct yourself and how you respond to client preferences.

You can exude **influence** over the efficiency within your team. Your level of cooperation, responsiveness, and unselfish contribution greatly influences project outcomes and customer satisfaction.

Unless you are high up on the leadership chain, you need to **adhere** to the majority rules of culture. But over time, your contribution on the individual and team level can have a positive influence here as well.

Regardless of your level of control, influence, or adherence, you will always enhance client interactions through awareness, a positive attitude, and proactive behavior.

Remember:

- The only person's behavior you can change is your own. If your client routinely shows up late, wasting everyone's time, ask what you can do to schedule meetings at times the client has fewer pressing demands.

- Avoid blaming the institution for disappointments in project outcomes. If your company's antiquated computer system accounts for delays and partial deliveries, suggest "work arounds" such as outsourcing some printing or scheduling heavy data entry early or late in the day.

- Always look before you leap—understand the implications of your behavior. If your enthusiasm to gather project data motivates you to directly contact all stakeholders on the client's side, hold off. Consult with your primary client representative *in advance* to be sure you won't be overstepping your bounds, violating client protocol, and complicating the relationship.

- If your choice of action will not improve client interactions, reconsider. If your response to a client's overuse of acronyms and buzzwords is to resort to the same approach, take a deep breath before you RSVP. Perhaps compiling a directory of technical terms and acronyms for the entire team will have a better impact on the relationship.

- Don't complain, offer constructive criticism. If a team member is challenged by the workload and always late with the deliverables you need, respond with suggestions for time management rather than negative comments.

FIVE MAJOR INTERACTION-BASED CAUSES FOR PROJECT FAILURE

There are dozens of documented causes for project failure. These causes can be due to technical performance, or service performance. On the technical side, the causes tend to be more explicit and easier to measure. On the service side, the causes are more subjective and difficult to pinpoint or define.

The five causes of project failure that result from poorly managed client relationships are:

- Unclear definition
- Problems with risk management
- Poorly managed hand-offs
- Untested assumptions
- Lack of communication (particularly around project changes)

These causes will be described briefly here and addressed more fully in the following chapters. Preventive and contingent strategies for managing these challenges will also be addressed.

Unclear Definition

Clearly defining the solution is often overlooked. The project team has a "gut feel" for what needs to get done, so they throw it into gear and move forward without a map.

A well-defined solution will involve many parameters of client interactions, including:

- What is the ideal project outcome; who will benefit; when and where will it be realized?
- What are the deliverables for the project?

■ What assumptions may turn into barriers?

■ Have boundaries and constraints been defined?

All these questions (and more) will need to be answered at some point during the project. The best time is upfront, before a negative impact on client interactions (and confidence) has developed. By choosing when to communicate and answer questions like these, you are managing rather than reacting to client requirements.

Problems with Risk Management

Risks must be identified and managed in all phases of every project. Best case scenario: risks will be identified and prevented. Next best scenario: risks will be identified and a contingency plan put in place in case the risk materializes. Worst case scenario: the risk is never identified, and when it erupts, the project is substantially damaged.

In addition to the technical risks that can plague projects (poor budgeting, missing milestones, incomplete documentation), there are also significant relationship risks.

Being implicit in most cases, relationship risks are tough to identify. For example, your project client may have serious confidence problems with a member of your team. Rather than express those concerns, the client avoids the individual, won't return calls, and perhaps tells others about his or her unfavorable impressions. This "chink in the relationship armor" leads to delays, uncomfortable undertones, and compromised project outcomes.

Diligent definition of relationship risks, and a committed investment to eliminate them, will increase any project's chance of success.

Poorly Managed Hand-offs

Hand-offs are the most explicit example of supplier/client inter-action in practice.

A well-managed hand-off is a *scheduled delivery* of a *defined deliv-erable* between *supplier and client* at an *agreed place* (computers and voice mailboxes included). It is the perfect example of how WHAT you do (technical performance) combines with HOW you do it (serv-ice performance) to create client satisfaction.

Late or partial hand-offs can quickly damage relationships. Perhaps you have experienced a situation in which your supplier failed to deliver an important report or schedule to you on time. This resulted in your failure to deliver a hand-off to your client (perhaps your boss) on time, and reflected poorly on your performance. In these situa-tions, no one wants to hear excuses as to why you are late; they just want the results. Managing hand-offs can therefore be a crucial com-ponent for maintaining relationships based on confidence and trust.

Sloppy hand-offs are like a bad game of catch. Was the thrower at fault? Was the catcher distracted? Perhaps the ball was off-balance. It can become a finger pointing exercise that has no chance of a con-structive conclusion.

Conversely, well-managed hand-offs are highly visible testaments to strong supplier/client communication and compatibility. Use them to your advantage.

Untested Assumptions

It is safe to assume that with every project definition there will be a litany of assumptions. There has to be. Assumptions are not created by projects—they pre-exist in the culture, policies, history, and relationships that surround the project.

Not only are assumptions a common factor in your projects, they are a common cause of project failure. The most unfortunate aspect of this situation is the overlooked ease with which failure could be avoided.

The problem with assumptions is they are "part of the landscape"; they "come with the territory." What you need to do is isolate assumptions, define them, test their validity, and take action to prevent them or prepare for their eventual impact.

You also need to be aware that assumptions can be based on technical performance (there will be enough money; the software will work) or service performance (we understand the Board's expectations; the project client prefers early morning meetings). Your challenge is to check out any assumption that may have high impact on your project and take action to minimize its potential negative influence.

Lack of Communication

Communication problems can upset individuals, relationships, and teams in every phase of project execution. You will see examples of communication breakdowns in each of the project phases.

A few examples of how a lack of communication can impede progress are:

Initiation Phase:

- Poor communication of definitions (scope, roles, solutions, etc.)
- Inadequate communication with high influence stakeholders and decision makers

Planning Phase:

- Incomplete communication of the plan to everyone involved in and affected by the project
- Lack of involvement of key players in the planning process (limits buy-in and ownership)

Implementation Phase:

- Poor communication around hand-offs (before and after)
- Undefined communication process between suppliers and clients

Close Out:

- No formal communication that project has been completed
- No process for communicating lessons learned and best practices

SERVICE PLAN

Technical aspects of a project are explicit deliverables—things like reports, budgets, directories, and tangible products. Building a project plan around these items and/or events is fairly straightforward and familiar.

The implicit aspects of service performance—things like communication style, professionalism, managing expectations and perceptions—can be far more challenging to define and therefore incorporate into a plan. This is a major reason why most project leaders and teams never address the development of a service plan to complement the project plan.

A service plan will give you a decided competitive advantage for several reasons.

- Service plans are not typical, and will therefore favorably distinguish your approach to managing projects.

- Service plans transform *assumptions* about relationships into defined *processes* that can be discussed, practiced, and improved.

- Adherence to a service plan facilitates efficient execution of the overall project plan, leading to customer perceptions exceeding their expectations.

Some of the questions you can use to organize the development of a workable service plan are:

- Which clients are the best candidates for a service plan?
  - Clients that account for a large percent of your business
  - Clients being served by two or more of your employees
  - Prospects who view strong service plans as a competitive necessity
- What tools will best support your efforts to serve your client?
  - How far into the project cycle is the client?
  - How many people are in the project client community?
  - What media or communication style does the client prefer?
- How accurate can you be in defining client expectations?
  - How focused can you be in probing client expectations and preferences?
  - How confident is the client that you will make good use of the information he or she provides you?

You will be presented with an extensive outline for defining service plans that will work for you and the questions you can use to develop the plans later in the book.

Chapter Two

2

Relationship/ Project Initiation

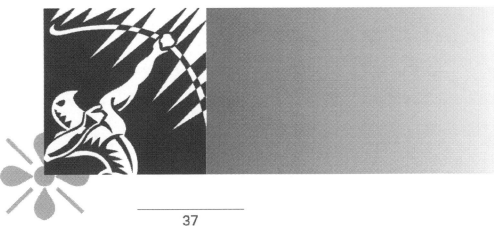

CLIENT RELATIONSHIP MANAGEMENT

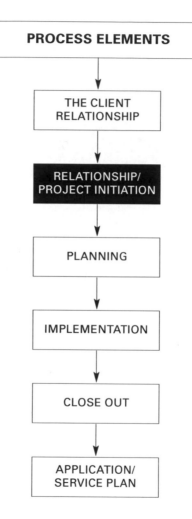

PROCESS ELEMENTS

THE CLIENT
RELATIONSHIP

RELATIONSHIP/
PROJECT INITIATION

PLANNING

IMPLEMENTATION

CLOSE OUT

APPLICATION/
SERVICE PLAN

WHAT? ✓ Relationship/Project Initiation

WHY? ✓ To ensure that every project/relationship begins with a clear understanding of client expectations around service level and interaction needs

HOW? ✓ Diagnose the need
✓ Define the solution
✓ Gain approval and support

KEY TOOLS ✓ Decision Matrix
✓ Tips and Reminders

CLIENT RELATIONSHIP BUILDING QUESTIONS

✓ What is the real need/problem/ opportunity?

✓ What are the service/relationship requirements?

✓ What solution will work best?

✓ How will we get approval/support needed to plan and implement the solution?

ADDITIONAL QUESTIONS

✓ _____

✓ _____

✓ _____

RELATIONSHIP BUILDING TIPS AND REMINDERS

1. Schedule all key stakeholders for an individual interview (in person if possible) before a solution is defined.

2. Learn all you can about your client's cultural history, outlining key events that led up to his or her present situation and needs.

3. Determine the client's preferred form and style for proposals (media, level of formality, level of detail, etc.) before documenting the solution.

4. Differentiate stakeholders as decision makers, influencers, and implementers and identify what each one expects from the project.

5. Determine which decisions and approvals require consensus and which do not.

6. Gain agreement from suppliers and clients on what will be measured and the measurement tools to be used.

7. Define a solution that will meet the customer's needs, then plan to over-deliver by adding value.

8. Use clear benefits statements in addition to tangible outcomes when defining the project solution.

9. Use terms and units of measure with which the client is familiar.

10. Know (in advance) the specific criteria that will be used in the approval process (by both decision makers and influencers), and address them in the definition.

REFERENCE MATERIAL
&
APPLICATION GUIDELINES

"We shape our buildings. Thereafter, they shape us."
—Winston Churchill

Think of the initiation of a project like pouring a foundation. It sets firm boundaries on its form and can seriously limit both the type of building you erect *and* the usefulness of it.

Remember, it is not just *what* you do but *how* you do it that leads to unrivaled project success. HOW you initiate a relationship/project sets a tone and a model for much of what follows, above and beneath the ground floor. Not surprisingly, this is where the success or failure of many projects is cast.

STAGES OF INITIATION

Your interaction with the client begins as soon as the client begins to formulate an impression of your organization. This can be from an initial conversation with a receptionist, reading an advertisement, hearing word of mouth comments, or experiencing the first direct contact with you. You may or may not have any control over the client's first impressions, but you need to be aware of them in order to productively manage the initiation of your project.

If you can safely assume some interaction preceded your involvement:

- Find out as much as possible about the previous encounters (who, what, when, where, and why).
- Determine what went well, and what didn't.
- If you uncover any pre-existing problems, make every effort to fix them without blaming or embarrassing anyone (you will be a hero to all involved).

Regardless of whether you are attempting to initiate a new relationship or expand one that currently exists, three stages within initiation always occur. There is no prescribed length for each stage, but there is a set order. It is:

- Diagnosis
- Definition
- Approval

These stages apply to project work as well as to all types of supplier–client interactions (including work with internal customers). Each stage has relationship management implications that need to be addressed.

Diagnosis

> "Don't ever take a fence down until you
> know why it was put up."
> —G.K. Chesterton

If you are entering the project very early on, you will most likely be involved with the diagnosis stage (i.e., figuring out what the problem, opportunity, or need actually is).

In the diagnosis stage, your goal is to determine why the current situation exists, or metaphorically, why the fence was erected in the first place. Invariably, this will require you to do some detective work, digging into the background and historical data that will develop into a clear picture of the events leading to the current situation. The more intellectual and emotional awareness you acquire about the client's relevant history, the better prepared you will be to craft a creative and effective solution.

A significant associated benefit is the client's increasing confidence that:

- You appreciate their evolution in arriving at this juncture.
- You respect their past and present cultural trends and influences.

∎ Your solution will reflect where they have been, *and* where they want to go.

In this stage, you are seeking to understand:

∎ Why does something need to be done *now*? (or soon)

 For example:

 ∎ Has there been an increase in new clients?

 ∎ Has there been an increase in client complaints?

 ∎ Does the business need to diversify?

∎ What events have led up to the current state of affairs?

 For example:

 ∎ Has there been a merger or acquisition?

 ∎ Is new leadership setting new priorities?

 ∎ Have market fluctuations required internal reorganization?

∎ What relationships are affected (or were affected) by these events?

 For example:

 ∎ Did relationships with existing customers change?

 ∎ Have internal relationships between departments gotten better or worse?

 ∎ Have reporting relationships changed for a number of employees?

∎ What previous solutions/alternatives have been attempted, and what do the results of these attempts reveal?

 For example:

 ∎ Can you draw from a repository of lessons learned or best practices?

 ∎ Have there been training programs directed at the situation?

 ∎ Have prior projects attempted to solve the problem?

∎ Do different opinions exist as to the need, opportunity, or problem? (i.e., are there two or more "camps" with competing ideas for solutions?)

For example:

- Are there two or more executives proposing differing solutions, or defining the situation in competing ways?
- Are there different solutions for domestic and international interests?
- Are there "old school" and "new school" forces in opposition?

■ Who are the stakeholders? (Identify stakeholders who "own" the situation *and* those who can influence whether or not a solution is pursued.)

For example:

- Who has the authority to interrupt or impede the project?
- Who will derive the most benefit from project success?
- What departments may not have an interest in the project but may be impacted by it?

■ What do key players believe to be the root cause of the problem?

For example:

- Will identifying the root cause have significant political fallout?
- Is the root cause strictly financial?
- Has the root cause been previously defined but ignored?

■ How well has the alleged root cause been verified?

For example:

- Is the data describing the alleged cause current and relevant?
- Is the person or group who defined the cause unbiased and properly trained?
- Have subject matter experts been called in to review the findings and verify their accuracy?

■ What relationships need to be carefully managed during the diagnosis stage?

For example:

- Are there any key stakeholders who may resist offering information important for accurate diagnosis?
- Will it be difficult to enlist the support of some key influence stakeholders who don't see the value of the project?
- Do you have access to key decision makers so you can determine how they will base their decisions?

Pursuing a solution or outcome without this vital information can lead to disappointing outcomes or abject failure. Part of your role as a relationship manager is to develop the client's commitment to honor best practices and lessons learned. This will impress the client with the value of his or her own experience and history, and your value as a facilitator of positive change. In particular, your interest in (and understanding of) key relationships will let the client know you are aware of the impact that these interactions may have on any new solution.

Definition

Have you ever entered a theatrical performance after the beginning of the second act? It can be challenging to catch up with the story line and get involved with the characters and plot.

This is often the case with projects. Clients tend to engage the services of project specialists once a problem or opportunity needs immediate attention and the first act (diagnosis) is over.

Some common reasons leading to your entrance at the definition stage are:

- The client has done a rudimentary diagnosis, but is not committed to the information or intends to use it in the definition of the solution.

- Time or budget constraints have forced the client to jump right to the definition stage with no investment in diagnosing the situation.
- Untested assumptions about their background/history lead the client to *believe* he or she knows the cause and therefore skips diagnosis.

All of these scenarios are less than ideal, and you will have to probe and sift to compose the clearest possible definition of the need, problem, or opportunity. At a minimum, you should solicit answers to the diagnostic questions, at least informally.

Even if your research falls short of giving you adequate information for a good diagnosis, it will help you establish relationships with key stakeholders and get the project off on the right foot.

If, however, the client resists spending any time on diagnosis, you may need to abort any attempts to explore the past, and rely on your judgment and intuition to get the most from the information you have. It's usually unwise, however, to put the project at risk in this way before it actually begins.

No matter at which point you become engaged in the definition stage, there is one key point to remember. The more accurate your understanding of the solution (and its evolution), the more likely the project outcomes will exceed the client's expectations.

Most clients will request that you document or package your proposed solution. This can be formal or informal.

Formal proposals usually require:

- A format specified by the client
- Submission requirements (number of copies, media, attachments, etc.)
- A specific process for submitting changes or revisions

Informal proposals can be:

▪ Written: letter, memo, or e-mail

▪ Prepared presentation

▪ Verbal "contract" in person or by phone (often followed by written summary notes)

The opportunity to submit a proposal is also an opportunity to develop the client relationship. Do your homework and find out as much as you can regarding the client's preferences in the items above, and prepare your proposal as close to those specifications as you can. This will demonstrate to the client that you are focused on his or her needs and committed to outstanding service performance.

Regardless of the depth or complexity of the proposal, it should include information gathered from the diagnosis stage, particularly as it relates to identifying the root cause of the problem. In fact, your proposal may actually help the client to rectify the root cause before implementing a solution.

Understanding and managing stakeholder needs is a significant part of relationship management. The definition stage is where relationship needs are interwoven with technical needs to craft a solution that can be embraced by the client.

Defining a solution requires answers to a few questions:

1. Who are the stakeholders? (Include those identified in diagnosis, and others as required due to the additional clarity of the definition. Remember, stakeholders can be decision makers, implementers, influencers, and those who are not involved but are *affected* by the project.)

2. What are the needs of the stakeholders for involvement and information?

3. Who will benefit from the need, opportunity, or problem being addressed successfully?

4. What would be an ideal outcome? (Where and when would it be realized?)

5. What would be delivered to whom and when as a result of this outcome being achieved?

6. Who will receive/use each deliverable?

7. Who would evaluate the success of this effort (i.e., which stakeholders)?

8. What will the evaluation criteria be? (What measurement tools or systems are currently in place?)

9. What boundaries/constraints must be respected during this effort?

10. What assumptions are being made about this situation and solution?

Comprehensive, clear answers to these questions will greatly improve your chances of exceeding your client's expectations.

In summary, the successful solution will be a composite of the input from the stakeholders, project clients, team members, and lessons learned (history). The more represented these players are in the solution, the more likely the approval process will proceed unencumbered. Managing relationships among key players will facilitate participation in the project and ownership of the outcomes.

Approval

A sound diagnosis and a comprehensive definition set the stage for a smooth approval process.

In diagnosis, the key is careful research into the organization's history. In definition, the key is a clear understanding of the client's needs and expectations.

In approval, the key is firmly based in managing relationships, and in knowing the preferences and decision-making style of all the stakeholders (which you have identified in the process of defining the solution).

In the process of establishing approval for the project, stakeholders fall into two major categories: decision makers and influencers.

Decision Makers

These people are usually high profile on the project, and they are consulted at all milestones and other junctures where "go/no go" decisions are made. They can be:

- The Project Leader
- The Project Client
- The Sponsor (providing funding, approval, or support for the project)
- Miscellaneous committees, boards, or managers who have a stake in the project's success

Influencers

While decision makers are fairly easy to identify, influencers may be obvious OR transparent in the project planning process.

Obvious influencers are the people who will use the project outcome(s) and/or those whose individual or department functions will be impacted by the project. These influencers tend to be well integrated in the project and part of the unfolding process. Though they may not make decisions, they are constantly using their authority to influence them.

Transparent influencers can be senior managers, longtime "vets" in the organization, and other core players whose position or history give them significant power over the company's culture. The influence these folks exert is not documented or directed at specific decision points. Its impact is both subtle and substantial as it shapes the way things happen more so than specifically *what* happens. You may not be able to pinpoint the source of their brand of influence, but you will certainly feel the impact.

The key then, to a smooth approval process, is to understand the needs, preferences, and expectations of as many stakeholders as possible. The better your understanding, the better your ability to manage the relationships.

Keep in mind that the relationships you have with your approval stakeholders can be multifaceted, and perhaps fluctuating. You may functionally report to a decision-making stakeholder as well as serve his or her needs relative to the project. Your relationships with influencers may vacillate from supplier to client and back again, depending on the stage of the project. The most important success factor is to keep these people involved by providing them with the information they want, when they want it, and how they want it delivered.

DECISION MATRIX

What:	**DECISION MATRIX**
Why:	To ensure that the needs of key stakeholders are considered when recommending solutions
How:	1. Identify goal and timing of decision.
	2. Identify stakeholders.
	3. Identify needs of each stakeholder relative to the decision.
	4. Identify current position on the issue for each stakeholder.
Where:	Blank template on page 61

The Decision Matrix is designed to help you quickly identify the preferences and priorities of the stakeholders who will influence and/or make the decision to proceed. Use it to organize and communicate your understanding of each stakeholder's needs and expectations.

The process of gathering this information from stakeholders will position you for a one-on-one interview in most cases. Whether by phone or in person, this is a golden opportunity to develop your relationship with stakeholders. Establish yourself as their advocate, representing their needs and expectations in the process. Be sincere and authentic. Create a rapport based on openness and candor. Initial steps taken now to earn the stakeholders' confidence will go a long way as the project unfolds.

The Decision Matrix SHOULD be completed prior to defining a solution. It MUST be completed prior to soliciting approval.

The Decision Matrix will help you focus on some pivotal questions related to approval of your solution:

1. What is the goal of the approval decision?
2. When does the decision need to be made?
3. Who are the decision makers?
4. Who are the influencers (both obvious and transparent)?
5. What criteria will be used to make the decision?
6. What is the current position of each of these stakeholders regarding the situation and/or the proposed solution?

If you answered these questions *during the definition stage* (along with the ten questions presented in the definition section above), you will have crafted a solution that completely addresses your client's needs. You have also set the stage for a smooth and uneventful approval.

If you answer these questions *while seeking approval*, you will successfully move the process along (best case). At the very least, you will discover any barriers or impediments to a smooth approval process.

Another important strategy for obtaining a fast approval is to respond quickly and completely to questions that were raised *by* your proposal as well as any other questions posed by stakeholders during the diagnosis and definition stages. Answer these questions promptly, preferably in writing, and with the appropriate level of detail for both decision makers and influencers. Remember that your relationship with the stakeholders at this juncture is defined by your awareness of and responsiveness to their information needs. Deliver a complete reply, on time, and in the preferred media and your chances for approval are greatly enhanced.

FIVE MAJOR INTERACTION-BASED CAUSES OF PROJECT FAILURE

Number One: Unclear Definition

There are several schools of thought among project professionals on what the phrase *"initial project definition"* means. Everyone agrees that the project outcome and deliverables must be defined, as a minimum. Some feel it is important to define the delivery schedule and an estimated budget before approval is sought. Others go the distance and outline a comprehensive plan, in addition to budgets and outcomes, before deciding a "go or no go" decision can be reached.

Your ability to develop a good relationship with your client during early discussions and through the diagnosis stage will determine how much influence you will have in recommending the depth of information required during definition. If you have used the diagnosis stage to establish yourself and the team as technical experts and top service performers, your client may simply require a clear definition of the solution to proceed. If your rapport with the client is shallow and he or she has not developed confidence in your team, he or she may require a lot more upfront information.

The more information you must compile before approval, the more resources you may be wasting. A tight, clear, accurate definition of the best solution for the client, based on a well-researched diagnosis, should be an adequate basis for approval of the project. It should also be enough information to make an expeditious decision to pull the plug on an ill-conceived project before the use of people and resources start running up costs.

If you have established a good relationship in the diagnosis stage, the definition stage offers an excellent opportunity to solidify it. Your proposal of a tight and focused definition should convey to the client that you are interested in meeting his or her exact needs and minimizing waste. On the contrary, unclear definition of the solution can lead to missed deadlines, budget overruns, stakeholder resistance, and a number of other problems, each leading to customer dissatisfaction.

In addition to being a pivotal element of project success, a clear definition can set a valuable precedent on how the client relationship will be managed and the project will be conducted. If the definition is hurried, poorly worded, or otherwise misses the mark, the technical and service performance on subsequent tasks may reflect this initial weak execution.

Typical Causes of Unclear Definitions

■ The client is not clear on what his or her real need actually is (a solid diagnosis could be instrumental in clearing this up).

For example, you are called in to stop a slide in profit margins for a manufacturer of resin-based patio furniture. The management feels a switch to more contemporary designs is the solution. What they haven't explored are solutions for the real need: to stop eroding profits. Are raw material costs too high—should they switch suppliers? Are inventories too large, adding to overhead? Are transportation costs eating into margins at an inflated rate? In other words, their need may have a much simpler solution than redesigning their entire line.

■ The client is not willing to take the time to describe the situation (he or she may take the stance that your job as solution provider is to discover his or her needs without his or her participation).

For example, you are reputed to be the best ad campaign consultant in the East. An importing firm calls you in to replicate their success in England with a line of tea biscuits, in New England. They have no interest in retracing their steps or giving you time to diagnose the situation. Your expertise is what they are buying and they expect to move forward quickly. Do you think a successful campaign can be launched without the benefit of a well-defined solution?

■ You and/or the client assume that the solution is clear and understood.

For example, you are a trade show planner for a software trade show that takes place every year in a major convention hall downtown. The past two years have seen reduced booth reservations through the fall, until you announce a price reduction and free amenities. This year the shortfall in reservations is the largest ever. You and the client feel it simply requires deeper discounts and better giveaways—the same as every other year. What you and the client have overlooked are an increase in similar shows in the area, the increase in e-buying for software, and the fact that fuel, lodging, and parking prices have doubled in the last five years. Will discounts be the solution?

■ The client is uncomfortable disclosing all the details for fear of breeching confidentiality barriers.

For example, you are put in charge of implementing a complete backroom payroll administration system for a successful privately held construction company. The CFO of the company refuses to release records on compensation history or current packages for principles and Board members. Without this information you cannot fully define the best accounting practices for the client, but he or she insists the project move forward anyway. Can you define a complete solution for the client?

Preventive Strategies

■ Use an informal event to initiate the *diagnosis and definition* stages (e.g., lunch, dinner, etc.). This may help the client to feel more comfortable about discussing the issues in question.

   ■ Discuss protocol around confidentiality. Agree to sign non-disclosure statements to make the client comfortable.

   ■ Apply active listening techniques to acquire information.

- Discuss how you can access other resources in the client organization.
- Develop the client's confidence that your methodology assures their satisfaction by proactively addressing issues that may negatively impact the project.
  - Describe your approach for testing assumptions.
  - Explain the benefits of risk management.
- Schedule a meeting to close out the diagnosis stage (including incorporation of stakeholder comments), and dedicate a segment of the meeting to confirm the needs of the client prior to initiating the definition stage.
  - Use the First Law of Service to assess the client's satisfaction with the diagnosis.
  - Seek input and clarification on the needs you have documented from all stakeholders.
  - Explore the client's preferences around proposal scope and sequence for presentation of the definition.
- Challenge the assumptions that you and/or the client have regarding the definition of the solution (see Untested Assumptions in Chapter 5).
  - Seek agreement on the scope and depth of the definition.
  - Probe for any insecurity on the client's behalf regarding competence of team members.
  - Present a list of assumptions you have made regarding the client's expectations, ability to secure necessary resources, time available, etc.

Contingent Strategies

- If the client is nonparticipatory, establish a process for the client to accept and approve (sign-off on) the definition that you have developed with the information you could gather. Include a detailed list of all questions and untested assumptions.

- Submit a clear and comprehensive proposal for the definition. This will facilitate approval as well as serve as a foundation document should subsequent disagreements or challenges to the definition materialize.

- Complete a Decision Matrix. It'll be very useful if any disputes or misunderstandings develop around the definition.

Due diligence pays off. Doing the homework required to produce an accurate diagnosis dovetails with the preparation of a clear and comprehensive definition of the best solution for the client. And remember, your homework is not limited to data gathering and technical research. You must be constantly promoting close communication, building confidence, and establishing a relationship based on teamwork and mutual support. The best evidence of great service performance at this juncture is accurate reflection of the client's needs in preparation of the clearest, most comprehensive definition possible.

DECISION MATRIX

Decision Goal:	Decision Timing: ■ Is there a date by which this decision must be made? _____ ■ If so, what happens after that date? _____ ■ If no, what time frame is realistic?	
Decision Makers/ Key Influencer(s)	Decision Criteria/Constraints (Go/No Go Factors) for each individual/group	Current Position/Opinion

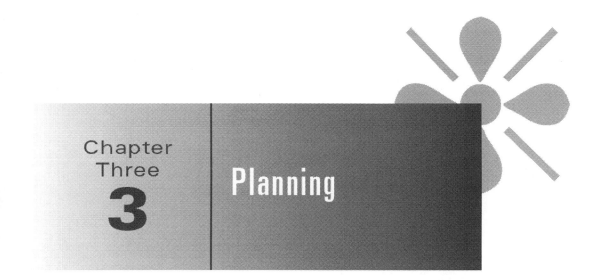

Chapter Three

3

Planning

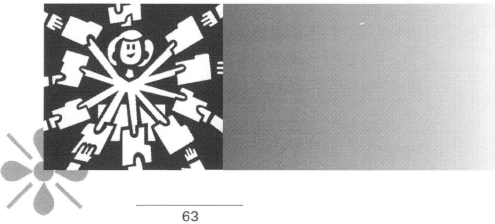

CLIENT RELATIONSHIP MANAGEMENT

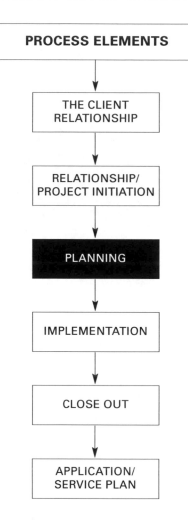

PROCESS ELEMENTS

THE CLIENT
RELATIONSHIP

RELATIONSHIP/
PROJECT INITIATION

PLANNING

IMPLEMENTATION

CLOSE OUT

APPLICATION/
SERVICE PLAN

WHAT?	✓ Planning

WHY?	✓ To build a workable plan that results in maximum involvement and buy-in

HOW?	✓ Complete Stakeholder Analysis ✓ Develop stakeholder buy-in for the solution ✓ Build the plan

KEY TOOLS	✓ Stakeholder Solution Assessment ✓ Stakeholder Issue Resolution ✓ Stakeholder Presentation Guide ✓ Commitment Summary/Action Item List ✓ Tips and Reminders

CLIENT RELATIONSHIP BUILDING QUESTIONS

- ✓ Who must buy-in to the solution?
- ✓ What is their assessment of the solution?
- ✓ How can we get them to support the solution?
- ✓ What needs to happen in order to implement the solution?

ADDITIONAL QUESTIONS

- ✓ _____
- ✓ _____
- ✓ _____

RELATIONSHIP BUILDING TIPS AND REMINDERS

1. Make sure all stakeholders agree on the planning process, have input (or defer their participation), and take ownership in the plan.
2. Set aside time early in the planning process to develop a risk management plan with the client, including preventive and contingent actions.
3. Provide each team member and customer with a folder of background information about the project and team members.
4. Consider potential "people problems" as well as project problems.
5. Elicit input and ideas from decision makers before committing to a plan, and schedule their time (well in advance) to review it once it's done.
6. Always acknowledge requests, questions, or suggestions by stakeholders, and commit to a time when you will respond to or incorporate them in the plan.
7. Allow time in a schedule for client review, sign-offs, holidays, and personal time.
8. Clarify why everyone on the team was selected, including his or her role, and ability to bring added value to the project.
9. Learn all relevant client acronyms associated with the project, and explain all planning terms and budgeting calculations before delivering planning documents.
10. Ensure the client is clear on his or her deadlines and handoffs, and knows the liabilities associated with missing them.

REFERENCE MATERIAL

&

APPLICATION GUIDELINES

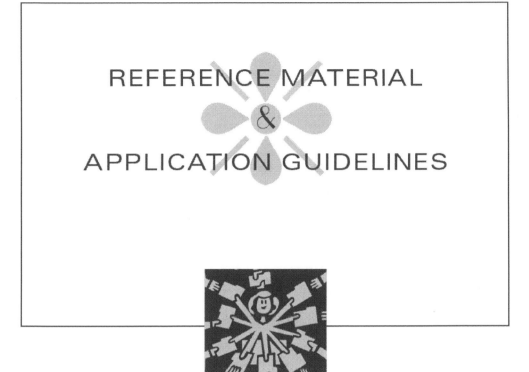

NOW WHAT?

> "The problem with Heaven is what
> you have to do to get there."
>
> —Unknown

This chapter is not about project planning. It's about making project planning successful.

You may also have heard the phrase "It is much easier to do than it is to plan to do." Our jobs and lives are so full that we feel compelled to keep accomplishing and just can't find the time to think ahead and get organized. We get caught reacting to fires rather than proactively installing the sprinklers. In projects, it isn't just important to create a solid plan, it is imperative.

By now you have:

- Diagnosed the current situation
- Defined the best solution for your client
- Received approval from key stakeholders

Now it's time to turn your attention to designing a workable, attainable implementation plan. A little forethought and planning will go a long way to avoid the pitfalls that accompany a "ready-fire-aim" approach to implementation.

The actual planning process is really quite straightforward. It simply describes the following considerations:

- **What** actions need to occur?
- **When** will each action be started/completed?
- **Who** will be responsible for each action?
- **How** much will it all cost?

Everyone On-Board

The real challenge in defining and holding to a plan is "keeping all the bayonets pointed outside the fort" during the process. Since most project teams are cross-functional in their membership make-up, there may be as many planning models in the team as there are members. For instance, Information Technology people may be familiar with a planning model driven by a sophisticated software program, whereas marketing people are more comfortable with hard copy calendars and spreadsheet forecasts.

The nature of an interdisciplinary team of people with diverse skills and interests presents you with a unique challenge as a relationship manager. This is the "formation stage" of team performance, and you must be prepared to hear all the input, involve all the players, and facilitate agreement on a planning process.

Pursue these steps with your team and the client:
- Agree that planning is key to project success
- Commit to a single planning model that everyone can use
- Apply the model consistently throughout the project life cycle

Below are five phrases which could define project outcomes in just about any organization. Experience with numerous project teams combined with survey input from hundreds of project professionals

Project Success Continuum

Shared Ownership   Disconnected Team

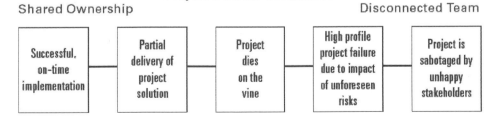

| Successful, on-time implementation | Partial delivery of project solution | Project dies on the vine | High profile project failure due to impact of unforeseen risks | Project is sabotaged by unhappy stakeholders |

suggest that the most influential factor affecting project success is shared ownership of the plan and teamwork to implement it.

Bottom line—your role is to pull the project off—on time, under budget, and exceeding client expectations. This can only be accomplished by carefully managing relationships, in the team and among the stakeholders, while keeping the project on track and up to speed.

RELATIONSHIP PLANNING

Don't waste time constructing a plan until you have thoroughly explored the needs and expectations of your stakeholders. We have emphasized the value of managing relationships with your stakeholders in previous stages, but it is even more critical here. If an important stakeholder hears about your project from anyone other than you, or at any time after planning has begun, you have one strike against you.

If a key stakeholder is taken by surprise, gets angry, or perhaps worst case, feels embarrassed by being out of the loop, the relationship that will be tested is with you. It is a test you don't want to take.

When the plan takes shape, it will include firm requirements for people and resources. This requires a budget, and that leads to spending. And when money starts getting spent, stakeholders pay close attention.

To remain on-board with you, they will need information in advance. Managing stakeholder information needs is a critical part of relationship management.

Some stakeholders are part of the core team and participate in every step of the planning process. Other stakeholders function on the project perimeter, and have roles as decision makers or influencers.

Regardless of their level of relationship to the planning process, *all* stakeholders must be consulted before the planning process begins.

STAKEHOLDER ANALYSIS

The rule rather than the exception is that some stakeholders will love the solution you have defined while others will find it unacceptable, unworkable, or simply ludicrous. Many projects have been scrubbed because a high influence stakeholder did not have a relationship with a project leader and felt they weren't given adequate opportunity for input in the planning process.

To find some balance or common ground, use the Stakeholder Analysis, which consists of two parts:

1. Stakeholder Solution Assessment (SSA): designed to identify what stakeholders do/do not like about the proposed solution.
2. Stakeholder Issue Resolution (SIR): designed to manage concerns about the solution voiced by stakeholders.

A good idea that never gets implemented is no better than a bad idea. When good ideas are implemented, the team wins, the organization wins, and the customer wins.

Good ideas emerge from open discussion and debate between suppliers and clients in stable, productive relationships. The SSA (Stakeholder Solution Assessment) and SIR (Stakeholder Issue Resolution) will facilitate this process.

These steps will lead you through a successful Stakeholder Analysis:

■ *Identify* all key stakeholders.
■ Conduct a Stakeholder Solution Assessment to *surface concerns*.
■ *Address concerns* through Stakeholder Issue Resolution.
■ *Present* to key stakeholders, seeking:

- *Acceptance*, then
- *Support*, and finally
- *Approval*

The objective of the Stakeholder Analysis is to promote a high level of acceptance of the team's solution. By doing so, the probability of successful implementation is taken to a new level.

Identifying Key Stakeholders

To implement a solution, it must be supported by the right people. You must develop strong and functional relationships with everyone who will approve, implement, be affected by, or simply support the solution.

The people whose support is needed are:
- Those who must formally approve the solution
- Those who must implement the solution
- Those who must live with the solution
- Those who must informally support the solution

Those who must formally approve the solution. This might be one person or a small group. Typically it is the person who has the final say. Budget and other resources may be involved. It then may be the person(s) with expenditure authority. Without formal approval, everything comes to a halt.

Those who must implement the solution. The people who must implement the solution must support it. Some of these people may be members of the team. It depends on the nature of the idea being proposed. There may be a number of people involved. For example, the team may have representatives from production, maintenance, engineering, or scheduling. Their solution may include changing the documentation for reporting on production output or machine uptime. The solution may involve others from these departments. It may also involve accounting, purchasing, and shipping.

It may not be practical to get the support of everyone included. However, identifying key stakeholders is critical. Key stakeholders are formal or informal leaders in groups or departments responsible for implementation of the solution.

Without support of key stakeholders, problems will arise. The end result may be failed implementation. Also, there may be a perception that the team came up with a bad idea.

Those who must live with the solution. The people directly affected by the solution are often those who implement it. However, they may be a different group altogether. For example, a team proposes a new office layout. The team will also be involved with implementation. Programmers, engineers, and others who work in the office will live with the new layout. They will not be actively involved in implementing change. Their support is important, however. Without it, failure is likely.

This group may not appear to have clout. However, they represent an internal customer. As such, their needs should be given strong consideration. This is most important when the focus of the effort is the external customer. It is the efforts of satisfied internal customers that make external customer satisfaction possible.

Those who must informally support the solution. This group fits none of the previous categories. However, they are still important to success. They are often referred to as "champions" or "advocates." They command respect within the organization. Therefore, their support is extremely valuable.

This group may include top managers with little or no involvement with the implementation. Or, they may be very much part of the solution. In either case, they have clear influence with people in the previous categories. In particular, they have influence with those whose approval is needed.

For differing reasons, these people must support the solution. Their support is necessary for successful implementation. Identifying them is crucial to identifying key stakeholders.

The Role of Influence

Projects do not run in a vacuum. In addition to the impact the project has on the people who are responsible for conducting it, every project affects other individuals, groups, and even other projects. This means that a lot of people in the organization will take an interest in your project, for a wide variety of reasons. And where there is interest, there is also influence.

Webster defines influence very simply: "the power to affect others." Your challenge is to identify the source of the power, and the intent of the change, in order to secure the success of your project. The best, and perhaps only, way to do this is to develop good working relationships with all project stakeholders. (The two sections that follow describe tools to assist in the process of documenting and dealing with stakeholder concerns).

First let's consider where influencers get their power. These four categories are not exhaustive, but cover the most common situations.

1. **Position:** Department Heads, Plant Managers, Account Representatives, etc., can wield significant influence through the power vested in their position. Influential moves by these peo-

ple will most likely come "through channels", i.e., visible and documented efforts to change the project.

2. **Competence:** Every project has its complement of subject matter experts. These people exert influence through advice and/or criticism. Their efforts can be upfront and formal (e.g., reports at project review meetings) or subtle (side conversations to influence team members).

3. **Affiliation:** Every organization has its share of unofficial groups and cliques. Individuals who have participated on previous high profile projects, been successful in winning large accounts, or are on the "fast track" may have the right affiliation to impact change in your project. They are most effective influencing other people who would like to join their club.

4. **Politics:** You can name at least a half dozen people (managers as well as individual contributors) who are "connected." These people have the ear of key decision makers and can exercise significant influence without ever speaking to you.

You cannot change the source of anyone's ability to influence or their intent to exercise that influence. What you can do is influence the influence. You do this by learning their interests and needs surrounding your project, surfacing any dislikes or concerns, and using the four dimensions of relationship management to dissipate any negative consequences their influence may create.

One last point—influence is not always negative or destructive. Developing close relationships with stakeholders will also reveal your supporters and advocates. The better you are at positioning your project for meeting the needs of these important people, the more you will enjoy their benevolent influence.

STAKEHOLDER SOLUTION ASSESSMENT (SSA)

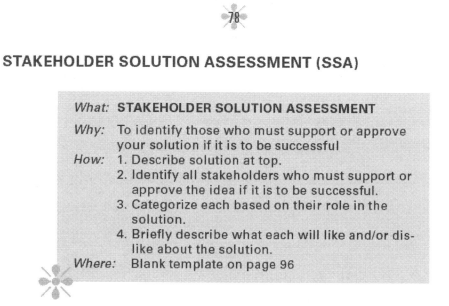

What: **STAKEHOLDER SOLUTION ASSESSMENT**

Why: To identify those who must support or approve your solution if it is to be successful

How: 1. Describe solution at top.
2. Identify all stakeholders who must support or approve the idea if it is to be successful.
3. Categorize each based on their role in the solution.
4. Briefly describe what each will like and/or dislike about the solution.

Where: Blank template on page 96

The Stakeholder Solution Assessment identifies people who must support the solution. It also identifies the parts of the solution that they may like or dislike.

Be receptive to suggestions and open to change during SSA interviews. This will strengthen your relationships with stakeholders and confirm that their needs and issues are driving the solution forward. This information is used later for presentation development. It may also result in minor changes to the solution.

As you gather feedback from stakeholders for the SSA, remain neutral and receptive. Stakeholders may be looking for your agreement as they define their dislikes for the solution. You will best serve your role as relationship manager if you openly receive their concerns, acknowledge their validity, and confirm your understanding of the issue. Don't take sides. You need to fill the role of the neutral arbitrator in order to maintain viable relationships with all parties. In addition, being sensitive to the ways stakeholders may attempt to exude influence (refer to the previous section) will go a long way towards understanding their needs and issues.

Generating a Stakeholder Solution Assessment

1. The team uses the worksheet at the end of this chapter. With it they identify people who fall into each of the key stakeholder categories. Each is categorized by placing a check in the appropriate column next to his or her name. In some cases, an entire group or department may be on the list. Do this only when it is likely that the entire group or department may have the same concerns.

2. For each key stakeholder, briefly describe (using key words) what the team believes she or he may like or dislike about the solution. This data is later summarized for use in presentations to key stakeholders.

STAKEHOLDER ISSUE RESOLUTION (SIR)

What: **STAKEHOLDER ISSUE RESOLUTION**

Why: To determine how the dislikes of each key stakeholder can best be addressed

How:
1. Using the SIR worksheet, describe the solution at the top.
2. Rate each dislike on the SSR on a scale of 1 (low) to 3 (high).
3. Enter the most important dislikes onto the SIR worksheet.
4. Determine how each liability or dislike can be removed or managed.

Where: Blank template on page 97

At this stage, key stakeholders have been identified. Their likes and dislikes regarding the solution range from inconsequential to important. Their favorable views may be used in a presentation. The key stakeholder presentation will be described later in this section. but it is their dislikes that we focus on now.

Since the SIR is a tool for surfacing stakeholder dislikes, it can also expose criticisms, differences of opinion, disappointments, and conflicts. As you can imagine, the stage is set for emotions to peak and interpersonal disagreements to surface. Your role as a relationship manager is to maintain an atmosphere of neutrality and common purpose, keeping all eyes focused on the flag of customer satisfaction. Your goal is not to avoid conflict, but to handle it objectively and constructively.

A few tips to keep the process on track and under control:

- Minimize use of derogatory terms in favor of constructive suggestions.
- Delineate between ideas and their contributors.
- Attempt to minimize the use of dislikes or concerns as a means to influence project outcomes for political or personal gain (see pages 76 and 77).
- Don't allow past conflicts to creep into the discussion. Remain in the present.
- Help people listen by paraphrasing points, requesting clarity, or asking individuals to confirm their understanding.
- If a serious conflict arises, ask if it can be tabled for the time being and addressed later.
- Any suggestions that address individual needs and do not contribute to the solution must be challenged.
- Remain receptive but analytical. Don't take sides or show bias.

And remember, as you deal with the concerns of key stakeholders, you are demonstrating your respect for their involvement in the project. Stakeholders will be paying close attention to the weight their views have in the issue resolution process, and this is a chance for you to affirm your relationship as their advocate and representative.

Using the Stakeholder Issue Resolution Worksheet

The team reviews the SSA. Each dislike should be rated on the following scale of importance:

3—**High:**	Dislikes which, if not removed or managed, make implementation of the solution impossible.
2—**Moderate:**	If these dislikes are not removed or managed, the solution may be significantly compromised.
1—**Low:**	These dislikes have limited effect on implementation.

In most cases, the importance assigned an item is dictated by an individual's position. Other factors that affect the importance rating include the number who share the view. Cost or scheduling issues that impact product and service quality are also factors to consider.

The team should list the most important items on the SIR worksheet. For each item listed, the team identifies ways to manage or remove the dislike. Removing a dislike means that the item is actually removed from the solution. For example, the people responsible for a solution object to working overtime. The team looks for a way to remove overtime as a part of the solution.

Managing a dislike means that it cannot be removed. However, its effects can be managed. By managing it, the solution can still be implemented. Using the previous example, if overtime is necessary for the success of the solution mentioned above, the team proposes ways to manage the situation. Those working overtime may be given bonus pay, recognition, flexible scheduling, or compensation time.

PRESENTATION TO KEY STAKEHOLDERS
A Tool for Winning Approval and Support

> *What:* **STAKEHOLDER PRESENTATION GUIDE**
>
> *Why:* To let all key stakeholders know about your solution and get their support and approval
>
> *How:* 1. Analyze the audience.
> 2. Brainstorm key points using the Stakeholder Presentation Guide worksheet.
> 3. Outline the presentation.
> 4. Make necessary assignments and prepare materials.
> 5. Dry run the presentation.
> 6. Ensure all details are covered for presentation.
>
> *Where:* Blank template on page 98

In most cases, you must obtain approval for solutions. The key stakeholder presentation is one method for obtaining approval and an important tool for gaining the support of key stakeholders. The presentation provides for face-to-face interaction in which the elements of the problem and solution are presented. These elements include the:

- Problem
- Proposed solutions
- Constraints
- Resources needed
- Benefits

The presentation situation is also a way to recognize the team's efforts. You can use the presentation podium to highlight excellence in technical performance as well as outstanding service performance. It can be a subtle but powerful medium to underline the value of good working relationships and their contribution to attaining the solution.

By completing the preparation steps shown before, you will greatly enhance the likelihood of strong buy-in.

Preparing for a Presentation

Preparing for a presentation requires six key steps. The presentation worksheet at the end of this chapter is a checklist to use when preparing a presentation. The team should consider various alternatives for each part of the presentation. Graphs, charts, and tables are useful tools for presenting information.

1. **Analyze the audience.**

   Determine who will be involved in the presentation. Next, analyze audience needs, concerns, goals, biases, and possible objections. The team identifies how to appeal to the audience.

2. **Brainstorm key points.**

   Identify key points to be covered in the presentation. Don't worry about the order at this stage. Just get the ideas out.

3. **Prepare an outline.**

   Using the Stakeholder Presentation worksheet, organize the team's ideas into a logical sequence. Decide which data best describes the problem and solution.

4. **Make the necessary assignments.**

   Determine what charts, visuals, and samples are needed. Assign responsibility for obtaining them. Also, determine who will make each part of the presentation. Make presentations a team activity.

5. **Dry run the presentation**.

Practice makes perfect. This is especially true in key stakeholder presentations. Focus on the introduction, the use of persuasive data, the benefits, and the conclusion.

6. **Ensure all details are covered for presentation**.

Review all assignments to assure clarity and make certain all aspects are prepared.

SUMMARIZING COMMITMENT AND ACTION ITEMS

What: **COMMITMENT SUMMARY/ACTION ITEM LIST**

Why: To summarize actions needed to maximize commitment for your solution

How: 1. Identify the commitment offered by each key stakeholder using a scale of 5 (high) to 1 (low).
2. Identify the actions required to maximize commitment of key stakeholders.

Where: Blank template on page 99

The purpose of the key stakeholder presentation is to confirm acceptance, gain support, and secure approval for a solution. The presentation is incomplete until this is accomplished.

Your role as relationship manager throughout the stakeholder analysis process has included interviewing stakeholders and incorporating their concerns in the final solution. This process helps to assure that all stakeholders accept the solution even before the presentation begins.

In most cases, the presentation attendees will also support the solution, to some degree. To get full support, some form of action may need to be taken. Providing additional data, modifying the solution, or obtaining additional approval may be necessary. It is important that any necessary actions be agreed to before the end of the meeting.

The Commitment Summary and Action Item List is a convenient tool for summarizing the commitment of each attendee. It can be completed by the team as a whole. The main presenter acts as the facilitator of this activity.

Each key stakeholder at the meeting is asked for a candid assessment of his or her support for the solution. This is identified as being (5) high, (3) moderate, or (1) low. Ratings of 2 and 4 can be used to indicate intermediate levels of support.

If a rating other than 5 is given by a key stakeholder, they may have some reservations or concerns. In most cases, these concerns can be managed. In such cases, the individual should be asked, "What needs to be done to move your support up to a '5'?" These actions should be noted on the action item list. For each action listed, a completion date and responsible party should also be agreed to and entered. Also entered on the action list are the initials of the person(s) for whom the action is being taken. This is to increase their commitment and support and to draw attention to the interdependent relationship the two parties are depending on.

In some cases, the action suggested may not be appropriate or realistic. It may be necessary to negotiate an acceptable action to generate the necessary support without compromising the solution.

PUTTING THE PLAN TOGETHER

Good planning contributes to sound relationships, and sound relationships contribute to good planning.

With the Stakeholder Analysis complete, you have accomplished these important objectives:

■ You have a good idea how to meet the needs of all your key players as you develop the plan.

■ Where differences of opinion exist, you have a process to resolve them.

■ You have established a communication process with all the stakeholders, a vital element in managing relationships and developing a sense of ownership in this group.

The plan itself can be simple or complex, depending on the nature of the solution.

In its simplest form, a plan will answer these basic questions:

1. What actions need to occur?
2. When will each action be started/completed?
3. Who will be responsible for each action?
4. How much will it all cost?

Have you ever spent hours working on a plan (e.g., business plan or household budget) and once the plan is complete, it ends up in a drawer somewhere never to be referred to again? People often go through the motions of preparing a plan, never committing to use it as their guide and monitoring system. If this happens in a project, chances of success drop dramatically. In order for a plan to be useful to the team it must be realistic and workable. This depends on a few factors:

■ Having the right people (i.e., stakeholders) involved from the beginning

- Matching the experience of the people doing the planning with the requirements of the solution
- Reserving enough time to do the planning properly

Preparation of the Stakeholder Analysis included your commitment to involve everyone in the planning process. Now it is important to keep that commitment and get stakeholders to take part.

Getting Stakeholders Involved

Your relationships with stakeholders prior to the planning process have been based on information exchange and some negotiation to arrive at a solution. Now the relationships shift slightly to require creative contributions and commitments to the plan. Our vision turns from the present situation to execution of future actions and strategies.

All stakeholders can contribute to the planning process in one or more of the following ways:

Suggesting ideas for the plan: Seek the ideas of those who are not able to (or desire not to) be involved in the ongoing planning process before you begin planning for implementation. Make sure they have confidence their input will be considered and they are not being paid lip service.

Working on the actual plan: This is the best way to secure commitment and develop a sense of ownership. Get those that have the time, interest, and ability involved and keep them engaged.

Reviewing/revising the plan: All those who make suggestions for the plan should be asked to review and suggest revisions for the document. It is always preferable to have people suggest ideas for and/or work on the plan as a condition for reviewing it. This minimizes the likelihood that stakeholders will enter the process after implementation has begun and demand wholesale (perhaps even arbitrary) changes to the plan.

Approving the plan: One of the most valuable outcomes of the Stakeholder Analysis is engaging decision makers (especially those with approval authority) early in the planning process. The more ideas and suggestions you can elicit from these people prior to development of the plan, the more likely you are to develop good relationships and secure their approval once a plan is documented.

Making the Plan Realistic: Task Estimating

Now comes the challenging part. Figuring out how long it will actually take to get everything done. There are a few things you can do to make task estimating easier and more accurate. Ask questions about the task before giving an estimate of time involved.

Some questions to ask are:
1. Is the task expected by a certain date?
2. What do I need to complete this task?
3. Where do I get the input I need?
4. What am I expected to produce as a result of completing this task?
5. Who receives the output from my task?
6. What are the requirements for the output(s)?
7. What other tasks are dependent on my task completion?
8. Is there any slack time surrounding my task?

By asking these questions of the appropriate stakeholders, you will demonstrate your commitment to a successful outcome along with strong communication and positive relationships.

Once you understand the nature of the deadlines and dates surrounding your task, you are ready to estimate. Use the estimating guidelines and methods described here that make sense for your situation.

Estimating Methods and Guidelines

- If you are not familiar, ask people who actually do the work or have done the work, for input.
- Get an objective, expert opinion (from someone who is not working on the project).
- Find a similar task in a completed project plan to see how long it took to complete.
- Allow additional time for tasks:
  - being done for the first time
  - that require support from outside the project team or company
  - that have caused delays or problems in the past
  - in which the inputs or outputs are unclear
  - involving groups of people working together for the first time
  - in which the people responsible or doing the work are separated by time and distance
- Make your best educated guess. Incorporate estimating methods:
  - Approximation or "Rule of Thumb" uses past or others' experience to come close to the actual or exact task duration.
  - Definitive estimating is based on well-documented data about types of work and may involve input from suppliers, subcontractors, or even estimating guides or manuals.
  - Best case/Worst case estimating is a technique used in the PERT project planning method which factors both optimistic and pessimistic estimates into a realistic estimate.
- When possible, have the estimate reviewed by a second, experienced person.

Pulling It Together

In summary, to create an environment in which planning will be effective and enjoyable:

- Make sure everyone shares a commitment to develop and use a plan.
- Select a planning model that everyone has confidence in, and will use.
- Survey all stakeholders in advance of the planning process for ideas, concerns, and to learn their ongoing level of involvement.
- Line up the right people whose experience coincides with the requirements of the solution.
- Keep everyone involved and informed—develop ownership of the plan:
  - Schedule focused review meetings with adequate advanced notice.
  - Maintain routine and efficient communications.
  - Respond promptly to any questions raised along the way.
- Make the plan realistic, with attainable estimates for the length of each task.
- Prepare decision makers for their role in approving the plan:
  - Solicit their ideas before beginning the planning process.
  - Schedule their time to review the plan upon its completion.

The planning phase is a great opportunity for relationship development. Use it to learn about important client needs that will serve you well during implementation.

FIVE MAJOR INTERACTION-BASED CAUSES OF PROJECT FAILURE

Number Two: Problems with Risk Management

The main reason that risk management is one of the most common causes for project failure is that it is ignored. Many people feel it is futile to attempt to prevent the inevitable. Others compare managing risks to herding cats—try all you want, but you will only end up frustrating yourself.

The truth of the matter is that risks can be managed, and their impact greatly reduced. This applies to risks founded in technical material (e.g., project schedules can be changed due to a threatened truckers' strike) as well as in relationships (e.g., the turf battle between finance and marketing can create dangerous delays).

A straightforward methodology for managing risks can be applied to relationships within any project.

Consider a project to develop a marketing campaign to launch a new product. The product being introduced is not important. The key issue is the dispute between finance and marketing which could kill the project and open the door for competition to gain first access to the marketplace. In this example, you need to work with the finance and marketing executives as your clients as you attempt to deliver a plan for the campaign.

Typical Causes of Problems with Risk Management

- The client is unwilling to spend time worrying about problems that have not yet happened.
- The rapid pace of events leaves little time for risk management.
- The client is unsure how to manage risks around relationships.

Preventive Strategies

- Informally, ask the client about any concerns relating to stakeholders
  - Competence
  - Availability
  - Relationships between stakeholders
- Ask about the likely causes for each concern.
- Brainstorm ways to remove the causes and document actions to be taken.
- When possible, meet with conflicting parties ahead of time to clarify issues and emphasize the importance of achieving the outcome.

Contingent Strategies

- If no preventive actions can be taken, advise the client that the relationship-related risks could impact the project.
- Adjust the schedule, deliverables, etc., as needed.
- Ensure that your problem management process is well-defined (see Chapter Six: Application/Service Plan).

Example

Dealing with risks can itself be risky business. It is difficult to discuss failure or disappointment, even in a conceptual or predictive framework. Do your best to keep discussions around risk management based on facts, not hearsay (for technical issues), and behavior, not personalities (for relationship issues). An example:

Step One: Assess the Risk

Finance believes marketing overspends and underdelivers, and is threatening to push for a severely reduced budget for the project/campaign.

- Describe the specific risk in detail.

   The Finance VP feels the Marketing Director fails to see the impact on the company bottom line of excessive spending on fancy materials, expensive pilot studies, and knee-jerk ad campaigns. The issue is a fundamental lack of confidence.

- Assess the probability that the risk will become a barrier to progress.

   The probability is assessed at 75% to a sure thing.

- Assess the potential impact on the project (low, medium, or high).

   The impact is high—the two executives can bring the project to its knees and the investment in the new product can be lost.

NOTE: Once you have assessed probability and impact, you can make a decision whether this particular risk is worth spending any more time on. A Low/Low risk should be tabled. A High/Low risk is also a candidate for the back burner. When impact is Medium or High, take a close look.

Step Two: Design Actions to Offset Significant Risks

- **Preventive Strategies** (Actions that will eliminate the risk)
   - Ask the Finance VP to define the information Marketing could supply that would reduce his concerns and free the funds. Seek Marketing's compliance.
   - Identify a high influence stakeholder who can mediate and bring resolution between the two executives.

- Do a careful diagnosis of previous campaigns to see if one or two precedents have caused Finance to overreact. Then get Marketing to describe why these events will not be repeated.

■ **Contingent Strategies** (Actions that will minimize impact if the problem occurs)

- Define critical target markets so if funds are reduced you can still hit prime audiences.
- Develop a communication strategy so manufacturing and distribution can quickly revise plans if the campaign will be scaled back.
- Identify a high influence stakeholder who can overturn the decision of the Finance VP.

This case has several interesting implications for you as a relationship manager.

■ The whole problem may be a personal battle between the two executives. If you can find a way to mediate this emotional conflict, the risk may evaporate.

■ The risk may not be a problem at all, but a misunderstanding created by poor communication. If Finance is filled in on the *real* results Marketing dollars have accounted for, their fears may be resolved.

■ You may not have the authority to intervene, so you might seek the participation of another relationship manager (senior executive) to resolve the conflict and prevent the risk from materializing.

■ If the problem does materialize, one option for saving the project (overturning the decision by Finance) can actually increase the heat between the two departments, potentially increasing risk for future projects. You need to weigh the current risk potential for loss against future potential losses.

Risks founded in relationships can be based on a wide variety of perceptions:

- Interpersonal differences
- Lack of trust
- Perceived competence deficiencies
- Availability
- Respect for authority
- Personality preferences

In many instances, the best approach is to encourage everyone involved to behave in a manner that will best serve the goal of meeting the customer's needs. A willingness to "bury the hatchet" and focus on the prize may be the way to deliver the goods successfully.

STAKEHOLDER SOLUTION ASSESSMENT

SOLUTION / IDEA DESCRIPTION: _____

KEY PLAYER	ROLE		What will each person like about the idea or solution?	What will each person dislike about the idea or solution?
	Support			
	Live With			
	Implement			
	Approve			

STAKEHOLDER ISSUE RESOLUTION

SOLUTION / IDEA DESCRIPTION: _____

LIABILITY (Brief description of "dislikes")	Importance High (3) Moderate (2) Low (1)	How can it be removed? (Preventive Actions)	How can it be Managed? (Contingent Actions)

STAKEHOLDER PRESENTATION GUIDE		
PART 1. Introduction/Goal Description (include Presentation Agenda)	**REMEMBER** • Get their attention • Tell them what you're going to tell them	**YOUR IDEAS**
2. Problem Statement	• Clear, crisp definition	
3. Impact of Problem	• Show why it's important • Show how it wastes time, raises cost, reduces quality, etc. • Use evidence, examples	
4. Solution	• Clear, crisp definition of your proposed solution	
5. Benefits	• Show benefits • Do they outweigh cost? • Use evidence, examples	
6. Request Action	• Ask for what you want • Summarize with emphasis	

PRE-SESSION CHECKLIST

☐ People Informed   ☐ Room Scheduled   ☐ Equipment Available

☐ Seating Adequate   ☐ Agenda Prepared   ☐ Dry Run Completed

COMMITMENT SUMMARY/ACTION ITEM LIST

Presentation/Meeting Date:_____   Reason for Meeting:_____

NAME	COMMITMENT/ SUPPORT LEVEL 5 = High 3 = Moderate 1 = Low

ACTIONS REQUIRED	For (Initials)	By (Initials)	Date

Chapter Four

4

Implementation

CLIENT RELATIONSHIP MANAGEMENT

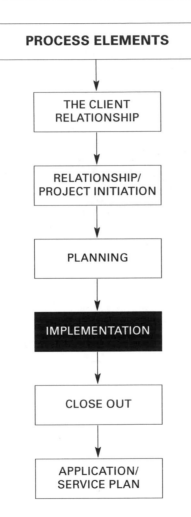

PROCESS ELEMENTS

THE CLIENT RELATIONSHIP

RELATIONSHIP/ PROJECT INITIATION

PLANNING

IMPLEMENTATION

CLOSE OUT

APPLICATION/ SERVICE PLAN

WHAT?	✓ Implementation

WHY?	✓ To ensure that client expectations are exceeded as the solution is implemented

HOW?	✓ Communicate the hand-offs ✓ Communicate clearly and often

KEY TOOLS	✓ Communication Matrix ✓ Tips and Reminders

CLIENT RELATIONSHIP BUILDING QUESTIONS

✓ Does everyone understand what they need to do?

✓ Have these needs been communicated to and agreed upon by suppliers (internal or external)?

✓ Does everyone understand and agree with the needs of their internal/external customers?

✓ How will we ensure clear, timely communication during implementation?

ADDITIONAL QUESTIONS

✓ _____

✓ _____

✓ _____

RELATIONSHIP BUILDING TIPS AND REMINDERS

1. Accurately define all hand-offs, make sure they take place on or ahead of schedule, and verify their successful completion.
2. Deliver client hand-offs in person whenever possible.
3. Help project team members manage their time and activities as planned commitments turn into actual tasks and obligations.
4. When briefing clients, discuss particular contributions by individual team members.
5. When hand-offs are missed or errors occur, pursue the root cause and appropriate corrective action rather than assigning blame.
6. Respond immediately when clients call with problems. Have contingent actions ready before calling whenever possible.
7. Notify all stakeholders as soon as a problem arises, solicit input on how to address it, and notify them upon resolution.
8. Maintain a personal connection with all stakeholders, and remain receptive to their suggestions.
9. Be sure everyone contributes during team meetings and encourage a balance between facts and opinions.
10. Encourage informal communication among stakeholders, and make people accountable for informing each other of "off line" discussions that affect them.

REFERENCE MATERIAL
&
APPLICATION GUIDELINES

MAKING IT HAPPEN

> "A fair idea put to use is better than a good
> idea kept on the polishing wheel."
>
> —Alex Osborne

Strong relationships require commitment and communication from both sides. Nowhere is this more true than in the area of project implementation.

Putting your plan into action will truly test your skills as a relationship manager. Documenting intentions is one thing; making them happen is another.

Anytime there is a requirement for a collective, coordinated effort among people who are not in a direct-reporting relationship, the "c C Phenomenon" shows up.

From Talking to Action

During initiation and planning, people are asked for their ideas, their opinions, their best practices, and to describe what they need as project participants. The dialogue is full of statements including phrases like "what if," "when we get there," and "we'll find a way." The atmosphere is creative and conceptual. There is plenty of excitement and no one wants to be left out of this high visibility, obviously important, initiative. People are anxious to sign on as participants and supporters, but only with a "lower case" level of commitment.

Then one morning, all the "small c" supporters get an e-mail, with an implementation plan attached. The plan is riddled with their name next to all sorts of tasks, meetings, reviews, and even trips. You can hear people thinking: "What have I gotten myself into? I never agreed to all this. I thought someone else would be assigned these steps. I haven't got time. How can I get out of this?"

Only when "small c" commitment gradually but surely grows into "capital C" Commitment can implementation succeed.

Your Role

Your role as a relationship manager is to make sure people accept their commitments. This will be more likely if they:

- Understand the diagnosis and what led to the current situation
- Agree with the solution that has been defined for the client
- Have developed ownership for and confidence in the plan
- Are clear as to their role AND what is expected of them as the plan unfolds

The last thing your project can afford is to have members and stakeholders bailing out during implementation. This is another reason consistent communication is so important. You may want to ask the following questions prior to final commitment to roll out the project plan.

- Do you fully understand what is being asked of you?
- Have you budgeted your time to allow you to make the target dates?
- Do you have the requisite experience to perform what has been asked of you?
- Has your supervisor given you enough flexibility to participate without penalty?
- Have any of your functional responsibilities increased since project inception?
- Do you know what to do in case your availability changes?

Asking these questions is no guarantee implementation will be pothole-free. It does, however, keep a fresh impression in everyone's mind of their value to the overall effort and their future responsibilities toward making it succeed.

An additional benefit of asking these questions is that you demonstrate your dedication to making each team member successful. It shows you are not only interested in the project outcomes but in the individual's ability to eliminate obstacles that may impede his or her personal performance. You are strengthening your role as an involved relationship manager, and as guardian of the service performance dimension of the project.

THE PLAN VERSUS REALITY

The project plan in many ways is a best guess. It represents a set of actions that you believe (or hope) will result in a successful outcome. The times associated with each task are estimates of what you think will be needed, given a specific set of conditions at the time. One key condition involves timely completion of predecessor tasks.

Given the fact that all task durations are estimates, it would be reasonable to expect that at least some of the tasks will take longer than expected. Unfortunately, you will probably not know which ones ahead of time. It is also reasonable to expect that other intervening variables (e.g., new requirements, quality problems, miscommunications, etc.) could further complicate things. Finally, it is unlikely, particularly with new project initiatives, that every necessary step will be accounted for (and in the proper sequence).

Once the plan is put together, it is up to members of the team to make it happen in spite of these formidable challenges. Specifically,

IMPLEMENTATION

111

it is up to each team member to manage his or her own tasks so that he or she contributes value to the project outcome. It is also up to each team member to test his or her tasks against the conditions that determine whether a task actually adds value to the plan.

By asking the questions on the previous pages, you can be a great asset to each team member and help him or her manage his or her respective tasks. You can also be an asset to the team as a whole by assisting in the management of relationships among team members:

- Encourage team members to maintain open communication with all other team members (formal and informal).

- When changing conditions impact a team member's task requirements or schedule, be sure he or she contacts any other team member that may also be affected.

- Keep team members clear on their client/supplier relationships within the team, and keep them focused on customer satisfaction.

Succeeding in Spite of Reality

In the initiation phase, people are *talking about doing something*, and asking these questions.

- Diagnosis: How did we get here?

- Definition: What will be the best possible solution for the client?

- Approval: Who needs to approve this solution, and how do I ensure it happens?

In the planning phase, people are *documenting intentions to do something*, and asking questions like these:

- Relationship Planning: Who are the key stakeholders and what do they need to see in the plan?

- Putting the Plan Together: How do I get the right people with relevant experience to apply enough time to get this done?

■ Making the Plan Realistic: Do all tasks within the plan have attainable time requirements assigned?

In the implementation phase, people are being asked to *deliver on those intentions*. With all of the obvious challenges, good communication and relationship management become essential.

One aspect of relationship management that is commonly overlooked is the definition of supplier/client transactions. We call this hand-off management. Anytime one person expects to take delivery of something (information, reports, product specs, airline tickets, etc.) from another person, a hand-off needs to take place.

The Hidden Magic

Hand-off management is the heart of any successful project. It is what turns the plan into a successful outcome, much like mortar is used to turn loose bricks into a wall. It involves connecting the people responsible for the tasks into a cohesive force that dramatically increases the likelihood that requirements and deadlines will be met. Specifically, it helps project team members to:

■ Achieve results that are clearly value added

■ Maintain a clear customer focus

■ Develop and maintain positive relationships with peers

■ Clearly understand how their individual contributions are connected to the project

A project is a true test of our ability in each of these areas. The more people on your team that exhibit these competencies, the greater your chances for success. Building a plan is one thing; making it happen is quite another. The foundation for making it happen is having everyone on the team manage their own relationships with suppliers and customers. It then becomes clear that relationship management happens at every level within the project.

While projects are managed by project managers, hand-offs are managed by project team members. The difference between simply performing tasks and managing transactions (with internal customers and suppliers) is what separates the successful project teams from the rest. Effective project managers are able to make this difference clear and explicit. (There is more information on hand-off management at the end of this chapter.)

COMMUNICATION

As you move through initiation and planning to implementation, the need for effective relationship management rises dramatically. Specifically, communication must be more frequent, clear, direct, and precise with each phase.

The Importance of Clear Communication Grows

The effects of poor communication are far more dramatic during implementation than they are during the previous phases.

Think of the information we need in order to execute a successful project to be like water. In the initiation stage, we are drilling for water—trying to piece together a clear view of the events that got us here. Once we have established a well filled with experience and history, we can then suggest a solution that addresses our client's needs. Communication of the solution is very important, but there are few interdependencies to worry about, and we can control most of the communication ourselves.

During planning, we are creating a new pool of information. Every stakeholder is asked to bring his or her buckets filled with information and pour them into a common pool of ideas, suggestions, and needs. The more we communicate with the project players, the more ideas we will have to work with, and the more comprehensive the plan will be. At the same time, if communication isn't the best, and a couple of people fail to make their best contribution, it probably won't make a huge difference in the outcome.

During implementation, we need to cooperatively move the information from one place to another. This requires teamwork and timing. Communication has to be exact and consistent. Each member of the team is like a length of hose, and has a responsibility to flow the information along, quickly and completely, as the project unfolds. Each coupling of the hose is like a critical hand-off. If one is missed, the information pipeline is broken and the implementation totally disconnected.

Communicate from the Start

Do you remember how it was stressed in the first paragraph of initiation how the success or failure of a project can be cast in concrete from the very outset? This applies to communication as much as any other aspect of project management.

If poor communication takes place during initiation (or any subsequent phase of the project), a precedent is being set. If communication bad habits remain unchecked, permission is being given to cut corners on future communications. As a relationship manager, you have a responsibility to model good communication techniques.

For instance, when it's time to define a solution for the client, a proposal should be developed. What if this proposal is poorly organized, full of typos, and hard to understand? What if it is delivered to you late and by fax instead of e-mail as you had requested?

This situation could inspire you to intervene and help the writer(s) do a better job, in the best interest of satisfying the client and setting high standards for the team. That would be a positive approach to managing relationships around communication.

If you choose to do nothing, and offer passive acceptance, you are in essence participating in degradation of the project. When substandard performance (technical or service performance) is unchallenged, expectations for excellence erode and project performance suffers.

Remember, communication takes many forms. These are just a few:

- Communication is what you hear:
  - Things said to you as well as things you overhear or hear about.
- Communication is what you don't hear:
  - Things that go unsaid can convey at least as powerful a message as explicit comments or instructions.
  - Don't assume that "no comment" implies "no opinion."
  - Lack of an explicit response can leave the door open for others to interpret or make assumptions on your opinions or position.
- Communication is what you see:
  - Behavior is a powerful communicator, setting examples and authorizing others to behave in certain ways.
  - Don't expect to get away with "do as I say, not as I do" in hierarchical or political situations. Your behavior provides evidence of your beliefs that words may not overcome.

As a relationship manager, you must be a model of good communication as well as coach for good communication habits in others.

Whenever making suggestions for how your team members or stakeholders can be better communicators, focus on the appropriate *behaviors* (e.g., "Perhaps you can mark your calendar to let Jim know a little earlier next time") and not on personal styles or *personalities* (e.g., "Your procrastination and late announcements make it difficult for Jim to do his part").

Reporting Requirements

In every project, there will usually be reporting requirements that are non-negotiable. These often include time/cost reports, change requests, and milestone progress reports. Find out what these are early in the project, and you will avoid unnecessary problems.

THE COMMUNICATION MATRIX (CM)

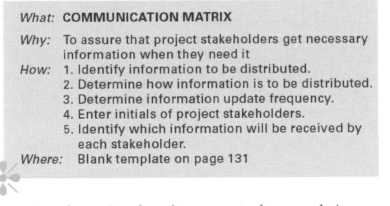

What: **COMMUNICATION MATRIX**

Why: To assure that project stakeholders get necessary information when they need it

How: 1. Identify information to be distributed.
2. Determine how information is to be distributed.
3. Determine information update frequency.
4. Enter initials of project stakeholders.
5. Identify which information will be received by each stakeholder.

Where: Blank template on page 131

As mentioned previously, a key aspect of your role in managing relationships is to encourage team members to be disciplined with communications. An excellent way to pursue this is the use of a tool for defining and documenting the expectations around communications of all stakeholders and project customers. The Communication Matrix is such a tool.

The Communication Matrix provides the foundation for a strong communication network. Along with meetings (discussed next), it helps to assure that important decisions are based on accurate, timely data.

The Communication Matrix allows for the distribution of data in a client-friendly manner. It allows each stakeholder to receive information in a format that best suits his or her needs.

The Communication Matrix allows project leaders and team members to get precise feedback on project performance in key areas. It also helps to assure that the right people get accurate information at the right time. Keeping all key stakeholders informed, in touch, and involved helps solidify interpersonal relationships, as well as commitment and support for the project.

To develop the Communication Matrix the project leader will need:

- Information Packages (any body of information relevant to the project)
- Information Distribution Method

    Hard Copy (H), Fax (F), E-mail (E), Meeting (M), Telephone (T), Inter/Intranet (I)
- Update Frequency

    Hourly (H), Daily (D), Weekly (W), Monthly (M), Quarterly (Q), Yearly (Y), Every 2 Weeks (W2), Twice per Week (2/W)
- Names (or initials) of the project team members who need information

Communication Matrix Contents

As projects become larger and more cross-functional, more data will be needed to manage the project. Thus, more data should find its way into the project file. For example, a large, cross-functional, multi-site project might require the following elements in the project file:

1. A cost/benefit analysis
2. A completed project scope summary
3. A project impact matrix
4. A project stakeholder directory
5. A milestone chart
6. Task lists and Gantt charts for each milestone (preferably in electronic format)
7. A summary of key hand-offs for each project team member
8. A project measurement summary
9. A distribution network
10. A meeting assessment summary
11. A risk assessment
12. A risk management plan

Communicating with the Project Customer

The most important communication you will have on the project is with the project customer. It is important to identify customer information requirements before the project begins or very early during implementation.

Whenever possible, you should make an effort to communicate with the project customer on a face-to-face basis. Communicating in person greatly expands the information you can gather, and allows you to tune and qualify your understanding of the client's needs interactively. Body language, eye contact, the setting for the discussion, tone of voice, and inflection—all these cues can enhance your ability to connect with the client. Face-to-face communication will also give you a better awareness of the client's preferences for being addressed and his or her comfort with interpersonal dialogue. All these factors will prepare you to serve the client in his or her preferred style.

In addition, opportunities for informal communication with the project customer should be exploited. These interactions can yield much useful information that is not typically available through formal channels.

Opportunities for informal communication include:

- Phone call "check-ins"
    - Short, "no agenda" phone calls to see if the client has any open issues or new questions you can address.
- FYI events
    - E-mails (perhaps with attachments), copies of articles, current events, even short verbal anecdotes that deliver information related to the project or your client's personal interests can spark valuable dialogue. These communications should add value to the project through the experience of others.
- Hand-off deliveries
    - Use every deliverable as a chance to engage in conversation related to the project or the specific hand-off. Since deliveries are usually moments of accomplishment, they can be unique opportunities to check on a client's level of satisfaction.
- Personal events
    - Get to know your client's birthday, anniversary, vacation plans, or other special events so you can express well wishes and/or offer congratulations. But be careful—we all know how the obligatory greeting or acknowledgment feels. If that is all you can muster, it is best to refrain altogether.

Managing Difficult Interactions

An important part of establishing an open and clear communication style with the customer is being prepared to deal with "bumps in the road." All relationships that are interdependent include some potential conflict or room for improvement.

Here are a few simple tips that may help you address those moments when the relationship hits a few waves:

1. **The Customer Disagrees.** This will happen, and hopefully you will *know* when it happens (a good relationship increases the chance the customer will express themselves). Whether the disagreement is mild or serious, stay focused and don't act defensively.

    a. Restate the customer's issue to ensure you understand his or her view.

    b. Acknowledge the validity of the claim.

    c. Offer information the customer may not have known, and which may counter his or her disagreement.

    d. Ask for direction or suggestions on how the issue can be resolved.

    e. Confirm steps you AND the customer will take to address the problem.

    f. Move quickly towards resolution.

2. **The Customer Gets Angry.** Anger directed at the project or the project team may or may not be rooted in the project process itself. REGARDLESS, the anger is real and you must acknowledge and deal with it. Your goal is *not* to qualify or defend against the anger but to dissipate it.

    a. Empathize, and apologize (saying "I'm sorry you feel that way" IS NOT accepting blame for the anger—simply acknowledging it).

    b. Explore possible causes for the anger. Agree on the most likely cause.

    c.   Offer solutions to remove the cause (if you have the control).

    d.   Offer solutions to compensate for the cause (if it can't be removed).

    e.   Offer suggestions for preventing the situation from repeating itself.

    f.   Re-focus attention and efforts on the project.

3.   **The Customer Gets Stuck in Minutia.** Customers can get mired down in a "nickel and diming" mode rather than moving ahead with the project. This may be due to their comfort in working with details rather than milestones, or a lack of ability to see the big picture. In any case, you need to maintain momentum. These tips may help re-focus the customer:

    a.   Acknowledge the value of attention to detail while reminding the customer of his or her value in managing the higher level issues.

    b.   Suggest the customer delegate the detail work to an associate and request a report on his or her progress.

    c.   Work with the customer to assign a date when the details will be put to bed and the customer will recommit to the project plan.

    d.   Align project resources to assist the customer in wrapping up the detail work as quickly as possible.

4.   **The Customer Asks for Changes.** Within reason, changes are a healthy thing. However, customers can become unreasonable with volume and frequency of changes. Changes are often the customer's way of asking for attention and securing control. This requires some adept relationship management, and possibly a delicate intervention.

    a.   Establish a change management process in which changes are explained, justified, and documented.

    b.   Make it very clear to the customer how changes impact the project schedule, costs, and affect other projects. (This is an attempt to make him or her accountable through objective means).

   c. Compare change requests to the original project scope summary to assess the need for or validity of the change.

   d. Avoid accepting changes to the scope without making adjustments to deliverables, dates, and costs, and making these adjustments known to all stakeholders.

In all four situations above, and the numerous other discrepancies that can arise with customers, the overall goal is to deal with their issues professionally, nondefensively, and with the clear intention of delivering the best solution. Because you are in a reactive rather than proactive mode, you should listen closely, accept the situation from the customer's perspective, and seek agreement for resolution—then move on.

A Simple Two-Letter Word

One simple two-letter word is often very difficult to say, in relation to projects and life in general. The word is *No*. The absence of this tiny expression of commitment results in some of the most damaging changes in project outcomes: scope creep, budget overruns, damaged relationships, and missed milestones to name a few.

Perhaps the most difficult situation in which to utter the No word is in response to a customer request. After all, you have spent lots of time and energy getting your customer to say *Yes*. How can you all of a sudden turn the tables and respond to his or her expression of need with a refusal to cooperate?

The truth of the matter is that there is no simple solution to this dilemma. Your role as a relationship manager puts you in the precarious position of keeping the customer satisfied while also keeping your project on track.

The most important aspect of how or when to say No is to exercise good judgment. Here are a few suggestions on how to prevent problems associated with not saying No. Each tip relies on your performance as a relationship manager and leveraging the rapport you have previously established with your stakeholders.

1. **Prediction Is Prevention:** Have a clear and concise discussion with key project customers and stakeholders (during the initiation stage) of the implications of changes to the project scope. Seek their "buy-in" to the reality that changes in the plan will directly result in changes in cost, delivery dates, quality, and overall project success. Orient them to the likelihood that you will need to resist or refuse significant changes if you are to act in the best interest of the project plan and deliver the defined solution.

2. **Yes Can Lead to No:** When a change is on the table, make concerted efforts to detail the implications of the change before accepting responsibility to honor it. If you agree to add deliverables, accelerate schedules, or reduce costs, your customer must simultaneously agree to alterations in the plan to accommodate his or her requests. This approach flips the coin so to speak, putting the responsibility back on the project client to retract the request or accept the associated impact on the project plan.

3. **Document the Situation:** In some cases, No is not an option. Key stakeholders (the project customer or your boss) may simply lay down the law and require that changes in the plan be honored. In these situations, take the time to document the change with complete objectivity, and describe the liabilities the change may precipitate. Distribute the "change bulletin" to all stakeholders.

Providing your project customer with a clear view of reality (i.e., changes do not occur in isolation—everything affects everything else) is not necessarily a negative event. In fact, taking the time (and calculated risk) to encourage a full appreciation of the implications of scope-changing requests may position you as a more valued partner and respected advisor. Using good judgment, solid communication skills, and relying on the facts will increase the likelihood that saying No to customer requests will improve your relationship with the client and confirm your ability to lead the project.

Communicating with Strong Influence Stakeholders

Strong influence stakeholders are people who do no value-added work on the project, but by virtue of their influence in and on the organization, can have a dramatic impact on the project (positive or negative). Like the project customer, strong influence stakeholders need to be kept informed regarding progress and results. This can be done by making relevant documents from the project file available during and after project implementation. It is also important to ask each strong influence stakeholder what his or her information requirements are.

One word of caution: Don't overload stakeholders with more information than they desire. It is a natural tendency to give stakeholders everything they could possibly want, with the intention of removing any chance they could complain about being left out of the loop. However, in today's information-intensive environment, piling on the documentation can be a bigger negative than holding back.

As with the project customer, opportunities for informal communication should be utilized when available. When appropriate, these interactions will help to solidify strong influence stakeholders' support. Equally important, you may learn of impending problems that might otherwise have escaped your attention.

Other Considerations

As you complete the Communication Matrix, keep a few points in mind:

- Stakeholder need for detail: how much/little detail is preferred by each stakeholder. Usually, the higher up the stakeholder is, the less detail required. Ask to be sure.
- Frequency of communication: how often each stakeholder needs to be informed about progress and issues.
- Communication method: how each stakeholder likes to be informed. While the Communication Matrix gives an indication as to the media desired, some stakeholders will prefer informal updates, while others will want more formal presentations.

In summary, consider how synonymous these three phrases are:

- Successful project implementation
- Successful relationship management
- Successful communications

Though not entirely interchangeable, you can surely see the deep overlap these terms have. Granted, a project may be successful without strong relationships, and outstanding customer relationships require more than good communications, but the connections are clear and undeniable. Pay attention to all three, and your project will progress naturally and deliver the greatest level of customer satisfaction possible.

Making Implementation Successful

Here are a few final suggestions for ensuring smooth implementation:

■ **Motivate the Team**

- Provide clear role definitions.

- Confirm understanding of future obligations.

- Assist those who need it with time management.

- Make sure everyone is Committed with a capital C.

■ **Do a Reality Check**

- Set realistic time estimates on all tasks.

- Plan for unforeseen or unaccounted for tasks.

- Establish a sense of responsibility in all team members for managing her or his own tasks.

- Validate all tasks as adding value to the collective effort.

- Clarify the supplier/client relationship and interdependencies (internal and external).

- Define and manage hand-offs for all deliverables.

■ **Be a Model of Outstanding Communications**

- Set strong precedents for good communication from the very beginning.

- Intervene whenever communications dip below standards. Offer constructive feedback for improvement.

- Prepare and share a Communication Matrix with all stakeholders.

- Be ready to clearly communicate how changes to the project plan will impact budgets, deliverables, schedules, etc., and say *No* to potentially destructive requests.

FIVE MAJOR INTERACTION-BASED CAUSES OF PROJECT FAILURE

Number Three—Poorly Defined Hand-Offs

Building a plan is one thing. Successfully executing that plan can be quite another. One of the most frequent causes of project delays and failure is the inability to manage hand-offs between project stakeholders.

One of the reasons so many project teams don't focus on hand-offs is that they are dependent, secondary events. In other words, a hand-off cannot exist until a supplier and a client define their individual responsibilities with respect to a certain deliverable. Project players commonly assume that clarity of these individual responsibilities is enough. What hasn't been confirmed, however, is everyone's understanding of how these actions will come together.

In this sense, a hand-off is like the corner of the room you are sitting in. The corner itself does not exist except for the coming together of the two walls. Contractors don't spend a lot of time worrying about or defining corners. They just "happen" in the process of building the room.

Don't assume hand-offs will just "happen," like corners, and you will have a far more successful project.

Typical Causes of Poorly Defined Hand-Offs

- Stakeholders don't communicate with internal suppliers and customers.
- Hand-off related needs are not clearly defined.

Preventive Strategies

- At each review meeting ask stakeholders to verify that they have everything they need (technical and service aspects) from their internal/external suppliers.
- Ask stakeholders to communicate with their suppliers, providing the what, where, and when for each deliverable.
- Encourage frequent formal and informal communication between stakeholders that have supplier/client interdependencies.

NOTE: Hand-offs are great examples of the truth in "it's not only *what* you do, but *how* you do it," especially when it comes to addressing client needs. Your clients can have very specific technical needs around hand-offs ("I want it in Word 6.0 format," or "Send e-copies to all my branch managers at the same time."). They can also have very specific (but implicit) service needs around hand-offs. You will prove yourself as a relationship manager if you can respond to service needs around hand-offs.

Some examples are:

- Would the client appreciate a personal delivery? Is there a specific person he or she would rather not see during a hand-off?
- Do you give the clear impression you are receptive to comments, suggestions—even significant changes?
- Are you consciously focused on surpassing expectations?
- Do you answer questions and respond to suggestions with a positive attitude?
- Does the client feel distinct and individually valued?

Contingent Strategies

- When hand-offs are missed, ask the affected parties to meet to clarify requirements, and commit to a firm delivery date/time.

(You may choose to attend that meeting because relationships may need to be managed.)

- Adjust project schedule/budget as needed.
- Advise the client on any imminent delays caused by the missed hand-off.

Consider this typical hand-off event:

This hand-off occurs within a project to produce a computer-based training course on the use of a new payroll-processing program for Perks Unlimited.

The project plan specifies that the team of writers will deliver the narrative for the first 100 frames of the CBT course to the editing team on the 60th day after project kick-off.

Unless discussed between the team members, these questions could interfere with a clean passing of the baton:

1. Does the 60 days account for holidays? Down time? Other interruptions?
2. Is the delivery via e-mail, zip disk, floppies, etc.? Is a hard copy included?
3. Where is the delivery to be received? On a certain desk? Onto a certain PC? Into a certain mailbox?
4. Is the delivery to be verified, formally (e.g., receipt) or informally (e.g., voice mail)?
5. If the delivery is delayed, how will the customer be notified?
6. Will associated graphics called for in the narrative be part of the delivery?
7. Is the project customer getting a copy of the delivery at the same time?
8. Is there an operating version of the payroll program available to check clarity of instructions?

CLIENT RELATIONSHIP MANAGEMENT

9. Who are the key contacts for Q/A after the delivery?
10. Is the editing team "clearing the deck" in anticipation of the delivery?

And there may be other systemic or project variables to consider. The point is, stating that a hand-off will, or should, occur is only scratching the surface. The parties involved must provide much more detail, isolate and test assumptions, and anticipate changes in the plan in order to maximize the likelihood that a hand-off will be successful. Developing relationships in which such questions are encouraged is a key part of successful projects.

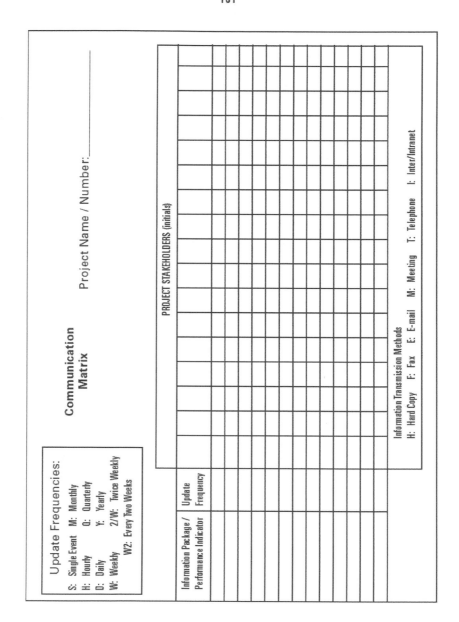

Chapter
Five
5

Close Out

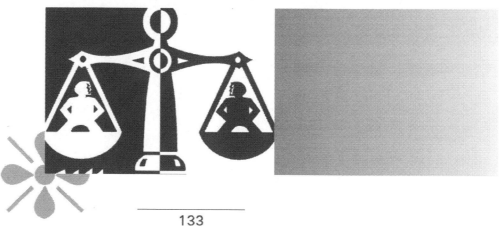

CLIENT RELATIONSHIP MANAGEMENT

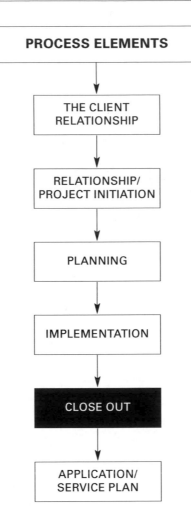

PROCESS ELEMENTS

THE CLIENT RELATIONSHIP

RELATIONSHIP/ PROJECT INITIATION

PLANNING

IMPLEMENTATION

CLOSE OUT

APPLICATION/ SERVICE PLAN

WHAT?	✓ Close-Out

WHY?	✓ To assess client satisfaction with the outcome and to identify new opportunities

HOW?	✓ Verify client receipt of the solution/outcome
	✓ Obtain client feedback
	✓ Review lessons learned
	✓ Identify new opportunities

KEY TOOLS	✓ Project Summary
	✓ Lessons Learned Summary
	✓ Relationship Extension Plan
	✓ Tips and Reminders

CLIENT RELATIONSHIP BUILDING QUESTIONS

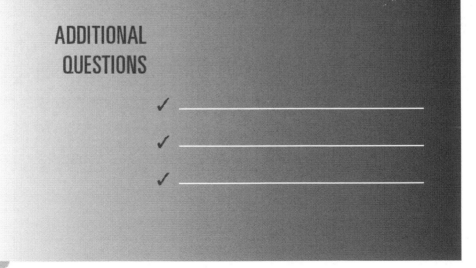

✓ Has the client received the solution/outcome?

✓ Was the client satisfied with the outcome/solution and related service?

✓ What lessons were learned during this project?

✓ What new opportunities can be pursued as a result of this project?

ADDITIONAL QUESTIONS

✓ _____

✓ _____

✓ _____

RELATIONSHIP BUILDING TIPS AND REMINDERS

1. Have the client verify (in writing) that final deliverables have been received and that the deliverables meet outcome specifications.
2. Communicate formal close-out of the project to all stakeholders.
3. Plan an organized effort to document, store, and distribute (if appropriate) lessons learned during the project.
4. Using the Project Summary as a guide, encourage the client to offer candid feedback on the interpersonal aspects of the project experience.
5. Follow up with management to acknowledge and resolve problematic systemic issues that surfaced during the project.
6. Schedule a review meeting to assess team effectiveness, focusing on Best Practices that contributed to project success.
7. Commit the client to a post-project interview for preparation of a Relationship Extension Plan.
8. Use measurement strategies that the client has pre-approved and understands.
9. Use a company communication vehicle (newsletter, e-mail distribution, staff meeting announcements, etc.) to announce successful project completion and appreciation for project stakeholders.
10. Seek out other individuals or groups in the client organization who may have interest in your (or the team's) services.

REFERENCE MATERIAL

&

APPLICATION GUIDELINES

THE WRAP-UP

"It ain't over 'til it's over."

—Yogi Berra

The end of a project can be the beginning of new opportunities. The responsibilities that come with project close out are as important as any that have occurred along the way.

Surprisingly, many project veterans have never experienced a phase they would label as close out. It seems the project simply fades away and the team quietly disbands once the final deliverable has been turned over to the client. No fireworks, no acknowledgment, and no closure.

Some reasons for this are:

- Project team members are pulled back into their functional roles by their department managers at the earliest possible opportunity.
- Project leaders are being pressured to move along to the next project.
- The project has been an interpersonal disaster and everyone can't wait to put it to bed.
- The project culture defines the end of the project as the delivery of the last element of the solution.
- Management sees no more revenue opportunities, so they pull the plug on the project and re-assign the team.

And there are many more possibilities. The important thing for you to understand is that project close out is a vital element of the current project, and it can have a significant impact on future projects.

Close Out Purpose

The purpose of the close out phase is to:

- Ensure that all deliverables have been received by your client
- Obtain feedback from the client
- Review project team performance
- Identify and begin follow-up on additional opportunities

When properly executed, the close out phase will wrap things up in a way that leaves the client with a positive perception of you and your organization. This may be the last and best chance for you to focus on the First Law of Service (satisfaction = perception - expectations) and truly impress your client by overdelivering. Remember that this is the moment of truth in your client's eyes, and never before in the project life cycle is the "what and how" of the delivery of the solution so crucial.

Equally important, and frequently overlooked, close out can be used to solidify and extend your relationship with the client. If you have exceeded expectations and the client is feeling he or she has profited from your work together, now is the time to identify ways to further develop the relationship.

And finally, close out is an opportunity for you to once more affirm your role as relationship manager within the team. You have the golden opportunity to:

- Acknowledge individual performance
- Acknowledge team performance
- Acknowledge stakeholder participation and contribution
- Highlight best practices
- Document lessons learned
- Confirm customer satisfaction

Any one of these close out communications can be rewarding and motivational to those who participated in and/or supported the project. If done well, they collectively will cast a bright light of success on the project and your skills as its relationship manager.

STEPS IN PROJECT CLOSE OUT

Verify Delivery of the Solution

The first step in this phase is to verify that the solution was implemented fully and effectively. It would be a serious mistake to rely solely on input from project team members in verifying solution delivery. Check with key project clients, and once you are satisfied THEY are satisfied, communicate the verification to all stakeholders. (See "Complete a Project Summary" as a way to verify client satisfaction with stakeholders.)

As a final step in verification, it is appropriate to request that the customer acknowledge receipt of the solution in writing. This document will become an important element of the project file, and may be very useful in extending the relationship with this client, or into other groups within the client organization.

Written verification can take many forms, from formal contracts to brief memos. Projects with complicated solutions may be served by a thorough checklist covering all key deliverables and the signatures of people who verified their receipt.

Smaller, shorter projects may only need a brief confirmation memo, on your letterhead and signed by both you and the client. (It is often a good idea to complete two copies of a confirmation document, leaving both client and supplier a copy with original signatures.)

143

SAMPLE CLOSE OUT/VERIFICATION MEMO

Date

Client Address

Dear _____ ,

Thank you for allowing us to be of service to you. Our entire team found working with you and your colleagues productive and enjoyable.

As promised, we have delivered all components of the planned solution by the agreed upon date of _____ .

The solution was reviewed and approved by _____ .

We appreciate your business and look forward to working with you again in the near future.

If questions come up regarding this or other solutions that you might need, please don't hesitate to contact me at _____ .

Sincerely,

Your Name

_____   _____

For Your Company   Date

_____   _____

Printed Client's Name

_____   _____

Received By (Client)   Date

Complete a Project Summary

> *What:* **PROJECT SUMMARY**
>
> *Why:* To obtain client feedback on project results
> *How:* 1. Inform the client (at project initiation) of the value of his or her feedback.
> 2. Deliver project summary to client for completion.
> 3. Review feedback with client.
> *Where:* Blank template on page 156

In verifying the client's satisfaction with the delivery of the solution, you are also getting confirmation that the technical performance of the team met or exceeded expectations. *What*, received *when*, and by *whom* is the tangible proof that the project solution has been completed.

Equally important (and perhaps more important for extending the relationship) is the client's satisfaction with the team's service performance.

Keep these issues in mind as you review the implemented solution and talk to a number of clients and stakeholders. You should know if the client offers any information in support or contrary to these points before completing the Project Summary.

1. Overall, is the client satisfied with the solution?

   ▪ Does the solution address all the criteria specified in the original definition?

   ▪ Do any aspects of the solution significantly exceed the client's expectations?

2. For each deliverable, would the client respond positively or negatively to:
   - Was it received in its entirety?
   - Was it delivered on time?
   - Did it meet all your requirements?
3. Did the client find it easy/comfortable working with our team?
   - Did the team communicate with the client according to desired parameters (how, when, where, etc.)?
   - Was the team reliable, accessible, and responsive?
   - Did the client feel involved at all times?

Essentially, the Project Summary is the team's report card. Questions 1 and 2 get the client's reaction to *what* the team did, and the rest of the information is feedback on *how* they did it.

The Project Summary is designed to provide an easy way for you to obtain this information from the client. It is a one-page summary that ensures that you have accurate and timely client feedback.

For best results, hand deliver a Project Summary to each project client as one aspect of the initiation stage. You can explain to the client that you will be focused on satisfying all of his or her needs and expectations, as evidenced by the type of feedback requested. This also "sets the switch" that he or she will be expected to provide feedback during project close out. Perhaps most important, it is an opportunity to draw attention to a dimension of your team that will distinguish you from the competition: the ability and intention to provide excellent service.

When it comes time to ask the client to complete the summary, it is a nice service to give each client a self-addressed, interoffice or stamped envelope for convenient return of the survey. Ask if a week is enough time, and if he or she has any questions. (Have extra surveys on hand for those who have lost them!)

If 10 business days pass and summaries are still outstanding, make a brief call or drop a note as a reminder to send it in. This information is very important and should be tactfully pursued.

Document Lessons Learned

What:	**LESSONS LEARNED SUMMARY**
Why:	To facilitate transfer of learning from one project to the next
How:	1. Complete project summary information.
	2. Agree on what went well.
	3. Agree on what can be done differently on different projects.
Where:	Blank template on page 157

Whenever possible, it can be useful to visit with the client during close out and discuss the effort in more detail. This can be a good excuse to meet casually, perhaps going out for dinner or lunch. Use this opportunity to level the playing field and work with the client as peers in a review process of the project. Assure the client that you will take no offense from his or her candid comments on the aspects of the project he or she would have liked to have experienced differently. Establish an atmosphere of objectivity and open reflection.

While you are no longer on the hook to deliver technical results, you are always being assessed for the delivery of service excellence. Assure the client that you appreciate and value his or her time, and you intend to make productive use of the information he or she is providing. And remember, your role is to ask open-ended questions, listen closely, avoid defensive reactions, and cement a relationship based on trust and confidence.

The clearer the client is that this discussion is intended to make you even more effective on future projects the more likely it is to lead to a discussion of future opportunities. If the conversation drifts that way, pursue it in the context of putting any lessons learned to productive use. When appropriate, confirm how your experience on this project allows you to be more productive (valuable and resourceful) on future collaborations with the client.

Though discussions of future potential are important and exciting, don't lose sight of the basic intent of this meeting: to capture valuable "Lessons Learned."

Every project is a repository of valuable information that can be used in future initiatives. Key information must be captured and shared for this to happen.

Information that should be shared:

- Project customer, purpose, and timing
- Responses to key questions
- Barriers encountered and how they were managed
- Major learnings from the project
- Major accomplishments
- Customer feedback
- Team member perceptions

In its simplest form, "Lessons Learned" should include a description of:

- Project customer, purpose, and timing
- What went well
- What the team would do differently next time

It is important to remember as you document your lessons learned that:

Knowledge eliminates mistakes and saves time. *Shared* knowledge eliminates redundancy and saves money.

The most innovative lessons learned are useless unless other project teams can learn from them. Put your experience to productive use by:

- Using every appropriate distribution channel to expose Lessons Learned.
- Submit Lessons Learned to whatever knowledge repositories exist in your organization or the client's organization.
- Incorporate Lessons Learned into your Project Summary, Relationship Extension Plan, and Service Plan, as appropriate.
- Refer to Lessons Learned when involved in any future project initiation efforts to validate diagnosis and definition with relevant experience.

Prepare a Relationship Extension Plan

What: **RELATIONSHIP EXTENSION PLAN**

Why: To identify additional opportunities to partner with satisfied clients

How: 1. Meet with client to discuss potential opportunities using the REP.
 2. Identify/agree on next steps.

Where: Blank template on page 158

Which of the following should be treated as a client?

∎ A prospect involved in evaluating the fit between his or her needs and your services

∎ A paying project customer

∎ A former paying customer with whom you have no current business

Obviously, all of the above. Most of this program has focused on the second type of client, the paying project customer. This section focuses on the former paying customer, and what you can do to increase the likelihood they will be a future-paying customer.

The cost of finding a new client is typically about six times as much as that needed to keep an existing client. Based on the financial incentives alone, you should be motivated to make every conceivable effort to keep every client for as long as possible.

In addition to measurable revenue, satisfied clients have tremendous value. These are a few ways clients can be important to you:

∎ They can refer business your way.

∎ They may provide recommendations for prospects.

- They may offer testimonials for your promotions and advertising.
- They can be a sounding board for new product ideas or marketing programs.

For each contribution above, there is no tangible benefit to the client. Yet it is a basic premise in marketing that any time two parties commit voluntarily to a transaction, they must profit from it. If you have excelled as a relationship manager, you will have developed a desire in the client to partner with you and to serve you in return for exceeding his or her expectation. The client's willingness to support you is evidence that he or she profits from the feeling of being a contributing partner in your business.

From Success to New Opportunities

Given the level of confidence the client has developed in your services, it is the next natural step to look to the future for additional collaborations. These opportunities can be working together on a project again, or they can be developing new business in other areas of the organization. If the client feels other groups will profit from a relationship with you, he or she will be the best spokesperson imaginable.

A simple structured outline can help you approach the client with organized questions and a convenient way to capture information. The Relationship Extension Plan (REP) will foster a discussion between you and the client about potential opportunities including:

1. From whom can a written testimonial be obtained?
2. In what way can this solution be extended to other parts of the organization?
3. What additional value-added solutions can be offered to the current client?
4. What needs to happen to move ahead on these opportunities?

The Value of Face-to-Face Meeting

Whenever possible, use the Relationship Extension Plan in the context of a face-to-face interview. This allows you the flexibility to add follow-up questions for more detail or to clarify information offered by the client. Leaving the REP behind for the client to complete alone will result in less useful and possibly incomplete information.

Stay in touch with the client's level of comfort in offering the information requested by the REP. If you sense he or she is at all uncomfortable referring you to other departments, drop that direction and focus the questions on his or her future needs exclusively.

Once the Relationship Extension Plan has been completed, you can derive many benefits from it:

- Include it in the Project File as supplemental information.
- Distribute it to key stakeholders as confirmation of ongoing management of the client relationship.
- Use it to reinforce the success of the project for team members and other implementers.
- Draw from it when you are defining or proposing additional projects with the client.
- Use it as a work in progress and modify it as players, issues, or needs change within the client organization.

FIVE MAJOR INTERACTION-BASED CAUSES OF PROJECT FAILURE

Number Four: Untested Assumptions

Home Life Assumptions That Can Hurt:

- What do you mean, I was supposed to pick up the kids?
- I thought you knew.
- You have the traveler's checks, right?
- Your mother is leaving Friday.

Work Life Assumptions That Can Hurt:

- The budget is approved.
- Bob from Accounting is on the team.
- The International Division's buy-in is a sure thing.
- I have a direct line to the project customer Sr. VP.

Assumptions are always dangerous. Assumptions can be based on:

- Past performance projected on current conditions
  - *"We wrote all the code for ABC Inc. in the same amount of time. It's the same application. Piece of cake."*
- "Best Case" scenarios you hope will come true
  - *"If everyone shows up and buys what they said they needed, we'll easily make our goal for the show. Relax."*
- Limited information blown up to be "all we need to know"
  - *"We know she is looking to outsource the back room stuff, and Jack gave us a great referral. We're in—who cares who else is bidding."*
- Rumors, hearsay, or "what if" gossip
  - *"Heard the new CEO likes racy jokes. When we see her, we'll give up our best stuff."*

- Cultural defaults
  - *"Don't bother. There has never been a P.O. over $3,000 approved in less than 90 days. It will never get off the ground in 6 weeks."*
- Limiting beliefs
  - *"If I thought my boss would even consider it, I would go for it. All I can do now is risk embarrassing myself."*

And there are lots of other reasons, too. The one common aspect of all assumptions, no matter what causes them, is they can really hurt a project *unnecessarily*.

Typical Causes of Untested Assumptions

- You and/or your client never ask about or document assumptions.
- The rapid pace of events leaves little time for surfacing and testing assumptions.
- Even if assumptions surface, and you have time, you assume you can't neutralize them.

Preventive Strategies

- Use the diagnosis and definition stages of the initiation phase to identify and communicate assumptions that you and the client have about the project.
- Build actions into the plan that will ensure that all assumptions are tested, either in advance of implementation, or as assumptions surface along the way.
- Ensure clear definitions of all deliverables, roles, and hand-offs.

Contingent Strategies

- If the client will not take the time to surface and test assumptions, document your assumptions and ask the client to review them with you.

- Ensure that your problem management process (see Service Plan) is well-organized to address untested assumptions that cause problems on the project.

- Quickly communicate problems caused by untested assumptions to stakeholders, and adjust the plan accordingly.

There are three types of assumptions that can impact projects.

Undefined Assumptions: These assumptions go unmentioned and never surface during the project unless they become barriers. You don't want to find out about them after they have had a negative impact on your project.

For example, you sense your project client has some resistance to meeting with your top programmer, but you can't imagine why. He is talented, friendly, and a good communicator. After several weeks the client refuses to meet him, and the project grinds to a halt. You later learn the client is allergic to his cologne, but too self-conscious to say so.

Untested Assumptions: These are assumptions you are aware of and probably have verbalized during initiation or planning. Unfortunately, you have decided to live with them as constraints or potential risks. You have chosen to passively hope they will go away, or at least have a very limited impact on the project.

For example: Your team lives in fear of missing a milestone. The last team that did was immediately disbanded and several "heads rolled" when Mr. Hatchet found out. So, you rush the work and turn in a mediocre report—on time. Turns out Mr. Hatchet cares far more about quality then meeting unrealistic deadlines.

Tested Assumptions: Once you define an assumption, test its validity. This is often as simple as asking a few questions or composing a few postulates.

> For example: A memo to the Mr. Hatchet (mentioned above) might read, "Our team has carefully researched our options and we cannot produce our best work within the current schedule. Can you meet with us to brainstorm possible alternatives?"

Assumptions are sort of like termites—eating away at the foundation of our projects. The undefined assumptions are like the undetected termites. We live in blissful ignorance of the damage they are causing, and only wake up to the reality of their impact when the floorboards fall away beneath us.

The untested assumptions are similar to the little holes we find in our baseboard or traces of sawdust on the cellar floor. Something is eating away at our structure, but we are too busy to explore or investigate. Ultimately the damage done is the same as with the undetected pest—the unfortunate difference is we had a chance at prevention.

Unlike the explicit actions required to exterminate termites, neutralizing assumptions deals with implicit aspects of relationships. Bringing assumptions to the surface, and then finding ways to test and manage them, can be a true test of your relationship skills. The most important thing to remember is to never ignore them.

Nothing is more discouraging to a project team than to have an apparently benign issue, such as an untested assumption, blow up and bring their project to an abrupt end.

PROJECT SUMMARY

Project #_____   Client #_____   Client Name_____
Project Name_____   Project Leader_____

1. Were project requirements delivered?

   ❑ Completely
   ❑ Almost Completely
   ❑ Partially
   ❑ Not At All
   Comments:

2. Was it done on time?

   ❑ On/Ahead of Schedule
   ❑ Late (no effect on outcome)
   ❑ Late (minor effect on outcome)
   ❑ Late (major effect on outcome)
   Comments:

3. Was it done properly (i.e., did it meet all Customer requirements)?

   ❑ Exceeded Expectations   ❑ Met Expectations
   ❑ Almost Met Expectations   ❑ Fell Far Short of Expectations
   Comments:

4. Customer Service
   Rate how well the project leader/team members demonstrated the following:

		Always	Most of Time	Sometimes	Rarely	Never
a.	Professionalism — Appearance, language, attitude	❑	❑	❑	❑	❑
b.	Communication — Asking the right questions/ saying the right things at the right time	❑	❑	❑	❑	❑
c.	Availability and Responsiveness — There when you need them — Gets back to you in a timely manner	❑	❑	❑	❑	❑
d.	Quality, Value & Timeliness — Understands/meets your needs in each area	❑	❑	❑	❑	❑
e.	Product/Service Knowledge — Knows the answers or where to get them	❑	❑	❑	❑	❑
f.	Customer Problems/ Problem Customers — Prevents most of them; manages the rest effectively	❑	❑	❑	❑	❑

General Service Comments:_____

LESSONS LEARNED SUMMARY	
Project Outcome:_____ _____ Project Customer:_____ Start Date: _____ Finish Date: _____	
What Went Well	**What The Team Would Do Differently Next Time**

RELATIONSHIP EXTENSION PLAN

Client Name: _____

Solution Successfully Implemented:_____

1. Level of Client Satisfaction
   (10: Outstanding; 5: Acceptable; 1: Complete Failure): _____

2. From whom can a written client testimonial be obtained? _____

3. In what way can this solution be extended to other parts of the
   organization? _____
   _____

4. What related/derivative solutions can be developed for the client
   organization?_____
   _____

5. What additional/new value-added solutions can be offered to the
   current client? _____
   _____

Next Steps

Follow Up With	Regarding	By (date)	Method*

Follow up Methods:
V: Visit   T: Telephone   E: e-mail   M: Mail   F: Fax   P: Presentation

Chapter
SIX
6

Application/
Service Plan

CLIENT RELATIONSHIP MANAGEMENT

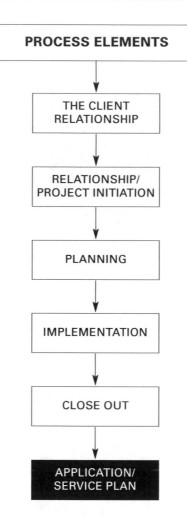

PROCESS ELEMENTS

THE CLIENT
RELATIONSHIP

RELATIONSHIP/
PROJECT INITIATION

PLANNING

IMPLEMENTATION

CLOSE OUT

APPLICATION/
SERVICE PLAN

| **WHAT?** | ✓ Application/Service Plan |

| **WHY?** | ✓ To ensure that the client's service and relationship needs are met along with the technical requirements of the project |

| **HOW?** | ✓ Identify key target clients
✓ Prepare service plan
✓ Communicate plan to affected stakeholders |

| **KEY TOOLS** | ✓ Application Matrix
✓ Service Plan
✓ Tips and Reminders |

CLIENT RELATIONSHIP BUILDING QUESTIONS

✓ Which clients need special attention?

✓ What will we do with/for these clients?

✓ How will we communicate these intentions?

ADDITIONAL QUESTIONS

✓ _____

✓ _____

✓ _____

RELATIONSHIP BUILDING TIPS AND REMINDERS

1. Use the Service Plan to make the implicit dimensions of service performance as tangible, and therefore, manageable as possible.

2. When the development of a Service Plan exposes conflicts or areas of contention, find the root cause of the problem, avoid assigning blame, and move quickly to resolve the situation.

3. Qualify your clients and prepare Service Plans for those that account for the greatest portion of your revenue or present other compelling reasons for the investment.

4. Employ the Application Matrix to assist in selection of the best tools and content for the client's specific Service Plan.

5. Encourage stakeholders to honor Service Plan commitments on a par with Project Plan commitments.

6. Brainstorm with stakeholders to define service performance components that will make the client say (and feel) WOW!

7. Use the information gathered in the Service Plan to closely manage both perceptions and expectations of the client.

8. Refer to the Service Plan for guidance on how to deliver technical outcomes in order to maximize client satisfaction.

9. Review the Service Plan at Project Review Meetings and modify it to reflect changing client expectations.

10. Use the Service Plan to confirm you are adjusting your methodology to client needs rather than expecting them to conform to your process.

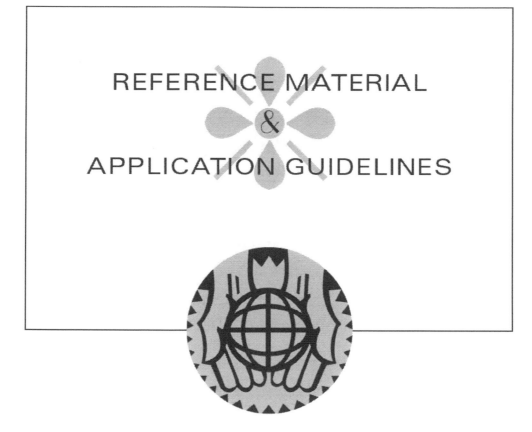

REFERENCE MATERIAL

&

APPLICATION GUIDELINES

PUT YOUR KNOWLEDGE TO WORK

"You can learn a lot from your clients. Some 70%
doesn't matter, but that 30% will kill you."
—Paul J. Paulson, President, Doyle, Dane Bernbach

There are many things about your relationship with your clients that are of marginal importance to your clients. There are other aspects that will be critical to their satisfaction. Learning which is which and acting on it could be the difference between a successful and unsuccessful initiative.

In a very general sense, a plan is simply the means to an end. The end is typically a good return on your investment.

Means (the Plan)	End (the ROI)
Business Plan	Work you enjoy; profits; security
Trip Itinerary	Relaxing vacation; time with family
Recipe	Tasty meal; good nutrition
Project Plan	Satisfied customer; profits; repeat business

Why then, do so many individuals and businesses overlook producing a Service Plan for their prime accounts? Surely the ROI at risk can be huge—conceivably the future of the business.

Don't Risk the Relationship

Your relationship with the client warrants some focused attention and planning. Your experience repeatedly reminds you that the way you handle the client can be the difference between repeat business and a lost account. Furthermore, you see indications everywhere that relationship management is becoming an essential element of successful suppliers. Seems like a compelling case for a Service Plan, but all too often no plan is produced. Perhaps these factors play a part:

- There is no process model or tool set for producing a Service Plan.
- The implicit elements that a Service Plan would address are too hard to define.
- There are no precedents in the business culture: it just isn't done.
- Service is not respected as making a contribution to the bottom line.
- The current level of service is apparently adequate—there are no complaints.
- There is too much to do and no time for the luxury of planning.

The list could go on. Notice that most, if not all, of the issues are "systemic" (i.e., aspects of the business culture or environment). That is a symptom of the fact that most businesses focus on technical performance and the logistics of delivering quality products. The businesses that balance their investment between technical performance and service performance will be tomorrow's industry leaders. These businesses will file Service Plans alongside Financial Plans, Marketing Plans, Business Plans, and Product Development Plans.

What Is a Service Plan, and Why Is It So Important?

- A Service Plan is way to organize your approach to the implicit deliverables your client needs, and to manage the "how" aspects of the relationship so client expectations are routinely exceeded.
- A Service Plan helps coordinate the efforts of an account team, keeping you in touch with your colleagues as you service key accounts. This will ensure adherence to consistent service standards and avoid embarrassing miscues.

- For key customers who account for a large percentage of your revenue, the simple presence of a Service Plan verifies that you value their business, and are willing to invest not only in delivering what they need, but in doing so in the way they prefer.

- The successful Service Plan will include techniques or tools for ensuring that the client's implicit expectations have been met or exceeded.

- Service Plans should be monitored regularly and adjusted along the way to meet the changing needs of the client and to be improved as your knowledge of the client grows. Good Service Plans are literally "works in progress."

- The most compelling reason to produce a Service Plan is the competitive advantage it will give you. The client may never disclose why he or she continues to order from you, but you can be assured that your consistent and visible commitment to service is a large part of it.

Inherent in all the points above is one simple yet compelling reason to develop Service Plans for your key accounts. Just as a retirement plan makes you think about what you need when you retire, the Service Plan makes you think about what your customers need in order to be satisfied by your efforts. Diverting your focus and energy from the tangible, technical deliverable to the implicit, service dimensions of your client relationship will result in a more balanced project effort and better performance overall.

Application Targets

Skills and tools are only useful if they are used. Every resource (including this one) must be put into practice in order to answer two important questions:

1. Does it work for you?
2. Can it make you more successful at what you do?

Before initiating any work on a Service Plan, think about these questions:

1. Do you believe a Service Plan will work for you?
2. Can it make you more successful at what you do?
3. Will your client have a positive reaction to a Service Plan approach?

Any new system, process, or set of skills must be field tested in order to determine its true value. Whatever you choose to use from this experience must receive YOUR complete commitment—only then can you affirmatively answer the first question noted above. As the manager of the supplier/client relationship, it is your responsibility to choose the right approach, the right people, and the right tools to service clients in a manner they have defined as right for them.

Not all projects and/or client relationships warrant the investment of a Service Plan.

The first step is to determine which projects and/or client relationships are appropriate as Service Plan application targets. Consider:

- Key clients that may account for a significant portion of your revenue
- Clients where one or more colleague will be working with you to support the project
- Prospective clients where a visible commitment to strong service performance could provide a competitive advantage for you

Application Matrix

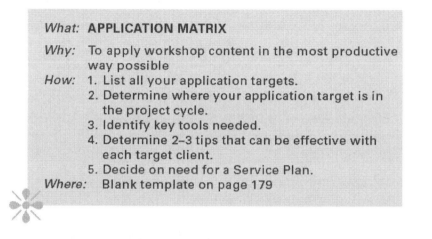

> *What:* **APPLICATION MATRIX**
> *Why:* To apply workshop content in the most productive
> way possible
> *How:* 1. List all your application targets.
> 2. Determine where your application target is in
> the project cycle.
> 3. Identify key tools needed.
> 4. Determine 2–3 tips that can be effective with
> each target client.
> 5. Decide on need for a Service Plan.
> *Where:* Blank template on page 179

In developing your Service Plan, you will have the opportunity to utilize tools and techniques covered in previous chapters. Choose them with care.

Not all tools and tips are appropriate for every relationship. The important thing to remember is to use what works at the right time. Don't "force fit" any process or tool where it doesn't belong.

The Application Matrix is designed to help you select the best tools for each of your application targets. For each application target, check off the tools that will help you to improve your service and relationship performance with that client. The last column allows you to make note of any tips and reminders that may be useful for relating well to each client.

It is likely that different tools and tips will be appropriate for different clients. Remember, the goal is to have your clients feel distinct and well-understood, not standardized or expected to conform to your process.

For example, one client may have already made a decision to proceed, so a Decision Matrix would not add value for you or him or her.

On the other hand, if you are working with a client with numerous stakeholders, a Communication Matrix will probably serve as a true asset on the project.

Bottom line, select only those tools and tips that will truly make your work easier, and your client relationships most productive. Avoid going through the motions for the sake of completing a form or engaging in unnecessary data collection.

SERVICE PLAN DEVELOPMENT

What: **SERVICE PLAN**

Why: To create a competitive advantage by ensuring client satisfaction

How:
1. Describe the project stakeholders and deliverables.
2. Identify ways to exceed client expectations
3. Identify client relationship management tools that will help the relationship.
4. Identify tips/techniques that will help the relationship.

Where: Blank template on pages 180–181

Every client is different. Each has their own expectations regarding service and relationship management. So, approaching each client the same way may have unwanted effects over the course of the project.

Every important client deserves a Service Plan. You and the team must be prepared to perform in response to the client's implicit service requirements as well as his or her explicit technical requirements.

CLIENT RELATIONSHIP MANAGEMENT

Development of a high quality Service Plan will require you to address a list of critical questions about your client. You will not sit down and answer these questions in a single session. Rather, you will address them as they come up while you progress through initiation, planning, implementation, and close out.

The more questions you are able to answer and act on, the greater the likelihood that you will routinely exceed client expectations on the implicit service deliverables.

1. What is the real opportunity, problem, or need?
   - Successful completion of the diagnosis stage of the initiation phase will answer this question.
2. Who are the players (decision makers, influencers, etc.)?
   - Successful completion of the Stakeholder Analysis in the planning phase will provide the answer to this question.
3. What are the primary deliverables?
   - Thorough work in the definition stage of the initiation phase (and possible development of a proposal) provide the answer to this question.
4. What are client expectations around professionalism?
   - How you look (casual dress, business-like, formal attire, etc.)
   - How you speak (speed, volume, acronyms, articulation, slang, jokes, use of titles, etc.)
   - How you act (casual, formal, professional, friendly, eye contact, body language, etc.)
5. What are client expectations around communication?
   - Frequency, timing, etc. (how often, time of day/week, how long per meeting, etc.)
   - Media (words, pictures, electronic, hard copy, etc.)
   - Transmission method (e.g., e-mail, phone, fax, etc.)
   - Level of detail (e.g., maximum, moderate, minimum)

- Asking questions (can you expect them to ask the right questions, or will you need to do it?)
- Data collection/distribution (who will do it—you or the client?)

6. What are client expectations around availability and responsiveness?
    - When do they need you (via phone, face-to-face, etc.)?
    - When and where do they like to meet (e.g., best days, times, locations, etc.)?
    - How long do they like to meet (maximum target duration)?
    - How quickly do they expect a response (may be dependent on the situation, although a default target can be set)?
    - How quickly can you expect them to respond (e.g., always, sometimes, never on time)?

7. What are client expectations around quality, value, and timeliness?
    - How many iterations are allowed before the final deliverable is produced (e.g., one, some, many)?
    - What value-added service/enhancements are they willing to pay for (e.g., none, useful, essential, etc.)?
    - How soon is ASAP (e.g., within an hour, a day, etc.)?
    - What level of client participation do they require (high, moderate, low)?

8. What are client expectations regarding your expertise?
    - What do they expect you to know about them and about their needs (low, moderate, high detail)?
    - What do they expect you to know about your products and services (technical expert, well-informed, basic user knowledge)?
    - What do they expect you to be able to find out/have access to (related information, resources, R&D contacts, other customers, top management, etc.)?
    - Where is consistency of information flow critical to client satisfaction (e.g., scheduling, deliverables, process, contacts, etc.)?

9. What are client expectations regarding problem management?

- Who will make initial contact with the client when a problem occurs?

- Who will follow-up after a problem has been fixed?

- Who will notify appropriate players during problem resolution?

- Who will manage any damage control?

- Who will ensure that the fix exceeds their expectations?

10. What can you do/provide (within the constraints of the relationship) that would make your client say WOW!?

- Will deliveries ahead of schedule impress or annoy them?

- Will check-in calls add value or be a nuisance?

- Will visits or calls from your upper management solidify or jeopardize your relationship?

- Are they very impressed with packaging or do they prefer to focus on substance?

- Do they enjoy having the relationship get public exposure or prefer confidential privacy?

- Do they prefer having connections with most or all team members or the consistency of one liaison?

The Service Plan template can be used to capture information about key client projects/relationships and will help you make the most of your efforts. Use it as a vehicle to ensure that everyone involved with these important clients contributes to a positive and profitable relationship.

Many people don't discuss the implicit aspects of relationships, never mind create a plan to manage them, because it feels awkward or uncomfortable. You have heard of the best friends who start a business and never develop a partnership agreement because they trust each other. A year later, the duo navigates a bitter partnership divorce. What they took for granted ended up destroying their opportunity.

The same is true for managing client relationships. If you feel by defining a plan you are predicting problems, get over it. You are doing exactly the opposite (i.e., defining a plan to do what you do better). A good Service Plan not only opens opportunities for exceeding client expectations, it demonstrates your commitment to meeting the explicit and implicit needs.

FIVE MAJOR INTERACTION-BASED CAUSES OF PROJECT FAILURE

Number Five: Lack of Sound Communication

Of the five interaction-based causes of project failure, lack of sound communication is by far the most common and the most devastating. A case can be made that all the causes of project failure come down to a simple failure to communicate.

In the interest of solving problems rather than being satisfied with identifying them, we have made poor communication situation-specific. Terms like "unclear definition" and "poorly defined hand-offs" are types of problems resulting from inadequate attention to communicating. If we have accurate labels for how lack of communicating can hurt projects, we have a shot at preventive or contingent actions to minimize the damage.

Similarly, most of the questions in the Service Plan and the Relationship Extension Plan are about communicating. Even the Tips sections of every chapter are there to focus your attention on tactics and strategies for being a better communicator.

At the risk of being redundant, this section will list some of the causes for, as well as ideas for preventing, poor communication. The more explicit we can make communications, and the nuances of behavior and emotion that surround it, the better we will be at getting the most from our relationships.

Typical Causes of Lack of Sound Communication

■ Communication is not encouraged, or modeled, by the project manager

  IF your project manager doesn't return calls or e-mails; sends memos full of cryptic technical jargon; never informs team members of changes in delivery dates—how will the team respond when they need to communicate? What will be the impact on customer satisfaction?

■ Stakeholders are geographically dispersed (by distance and/or time)

IF you send an e-mail to London at noon EST that a key project decision will be made by 6 PM today, EST, and their input is critical—what will the reply be? How important will your London stakeholders feel?

■ No time is allocated for formal project communication

IF it is assumed by project leaders that everyone is "in touch" with each other and there is no need for review meetings, progress summaries, or other status and update reports—what will happen to project coordination? Will the client know where the deliverables are in the project cycle?

■ No emphasis is placed on the value of informal communication

IF ad hoc meetings, spontaneous brainstorming sessions, and "drop by" conversations about project activities are discouraged in favor of "real work"—how informed will team members be of each other's progress? What will the impact be on creativity and project enjoyment among the team?

■ Meeting management skills are poor

IF meetings start late, run long, are not documented, and the wrong people are invited—how does that reflect on the overall importance of the project? What happens to team member relationships?

■ No mechanism exists for systematic information distribution to stakeholders (solved by use of the Communication Matrix)

IF stakeholders are not informed on project progress, or they hear about significant project events from nonproject sources—how will this affect their support for the project? How will strong influence stakeholders react to poor, late, or inaccurate communications?

■ Changes occur and all affected stakeholders are not informed

IF changes in project deliverables are not quickly and clearly communicated to all stakeholders, and those expecting the delivery assume everything is going according to plan—what happens to project effectiveness and interpersonal relationships when the delivery doesn't show up? How is stakeholder confidence in the project team affected?

Preventive Strategies

- When possible, develop a project web site for disseminating project information.

- Assign a "communications coach" for the team—select someone who values and is adept at clear, consistent communication (does not have to be the project manager).

- Build frequent (but short and to the point) review meetings into the project plan.

- Use a facilitator and a process to ensure meeting effectiveness.

- Facilitate opportunities for stakeholders to communicate informally (e.g., social events, team lunches, etc.).

- Incorporate a change management process that includes immediate communication to affected stakeholders.

Contingent Strategies

- Schedule periodic "issues" meetings to discuss and resolve communication-related problems. Develop an attitude that surfacing conflicts is an opportunity to improve performance.

- Ensure that the problem management process is designed to address problems associated with miscommunication.

APPLICATION MATRIX

Service Plan Required?																		
CRM TIPS Identify (by tip #) 2–3 tips for use with each application target																		
Relationship Extension Plan (p. 149)																		
Lessons Learned Summary (p. 146)																		
Project Summary (p. 144)																		
Communication Matrix (p. 116)																		
Commitment Summary/ Action Item List (p. 84)																		
Stakeholder Presentation Guide (p. 82)																		
Stakeholder Issue Resolution (p. 79)																		
Stakeholder Solution Assessment (p. 78)																		
Decision Matrix (p. 53)																		
APPLICATION TARGETS (Project/Relationship)																		

CLIENT RELATIONSHIP MANAGEMENT TOOLS

SERVICE PLAN

Client Name: _____ Phone: _____ Plan Date: _____

Client Contact: _____ e-mail: _____

What is the real opportunity, problem, or need?

_____

_____

Who are the players (decision makers, influencers, etc.)?

_____   _____

_____   _____

_____   _____

What are the primary deliverables?

_____   _____

_____   _____

What will we do to exceed client expectations around professionalism?

_____

_____

What will we do to exceed client expectations around communication?

_____

_____

What will we do to exceed client expectations around availability and responsiveness?

_____

_____

What will we do to exceed client expectations around quality, value, and timeliness?

_____

_____

What will we do to exceed client expectations regarding our expertise?

_____

_____

SERVICE PLAN *(continued)*

What will we do to exceed client expectations regarding problem management?

_____

_____

What can we do/provide (within the constraints of the relationship) that would make the client say WOW!?

_____

_____

Tools	Target Completion Date	Who
• Decision Matrix	_____	_____
• Stakeholder Analysis	_____	_____
• Presentation Guide	_____	_____
• Communication Matrix	_____	_____
• Project Summary	_____	_____
• Lessons Learned Summary	_____	_____
• Relationship Extension Plan	_____	_____

Project/Relationship Notes

Enter any ideas, tips, techniques that will aid in maintaining a positive relationship during each phase of the effort with this client.

Initiation: _____

_____

Planning: _____

_____

Implementation: _____

_____

Close Out: _____

_____

ABOUT THE AUTHOR

Dave Po-Chedley has been actively involved in improving organization effectiveness for over 20 years. He is currently President of Cambridge Consulting, Inc., and continues to work with clients around the world to enhance their effectiveness.

Thousands of people from organizations in North America, Europe, Asia, and South America have benefited from workshops and consulting services provided by Mr. Po-Chedley. They include:

Morgan Stanley Dean Witter
Johnson & Johnson
Florida Power and Light
FleetBoston Financial
General Electric
MITRE Corporation
All Children's Hospital of Florida
Bell Communications Research
World University Games
Pacific Gas and Electric
McDonnell Douglas Finance Company
Automobile Club of Michigan
Rich Products Corporation
OppenheimerFund
General Motors
Xerox
General Dynamics
US Airways
Harley Davidson

Boeing
Pratt & Whitney
Hewlett Packard
IBM
Kohler Company
Tenneco
AT&T
Bank of America

After earning an MS in Industrial Psychology at University of California, Long Beach, California, Dave worked at McDonnell-Douglas for 8 years as an employee and later as a consultant. During this time, he managed advanced flight deck research projects, and later, the Engineering Management Development function. In addition to developing and conducting a wide variety of management development workshops, Dave was involved with a number of organization change initiatives.

In 1983, Mr. Po-Chedley began working as a consultant to organizations in both the public and private sectors. During that time, he has helped a variety of Fortune 500 companies to improve their performance in the areas of project management, client relationship management, customer service, coaching, team effectiveness, problem solving, decision making, quality, productivity, and conflict management. He has authored workbooks and developed course materials in each of these areas for use in many fields including information systems, financial services, high technology, pharmaceuticals, and manufacturing.

Mr. Po-Chedley serves on the Board of Directors for Pioneer Aerospace, a supplier of deceleration equipment to the U.S. military, NASA, and foreign governments. He is also an active member of

ASTD (American Society of Training and Development) and PMI (Project Management Institute).

Related Services from Cambridge Consulting

For information about conducting in-house Client Relationship Management workshops in your organization, contact Cambridge Consulting at 800-621-5202 or 401-782-9222, or visit their web site at www.CambridgeConsult.com

Workshops and support services offered by Cambridge Consulting include:

- Client Relationship Management (one-day workshop)
- Project Management (one-, two-, and three-day workshops: basic, intermediate, advanced)
- E Projects: Issues and Solutions (one-day workshop)
- Managing Problems and Decisions (one- and two-day workshops)
- Customer Service Excellence (one-day workshop)
- Coaching (one-day workshop)
- Customer Servey Development and Administration
- Project Strategy Sessions (to address systemic and environmental barriers to project success)
- On-Site Project, Customer Service, and Client Relationship Consulting